20 Maresfield Gardens

20 Maresfield Gardens

A GUIDE TO THE FREUD MUSEUM LONDON

The Freud Museum

Library of Congress Catalog Card Number: 98-86083

A catalogue record for this book is available from
the British Library on request

The right of The Freud Museum Staff to be identified as
the authors of this work has been asserted by them in accordance
with the Copyright, Designs and Patents Act 1988

First published in 1998 by
Serpent's Tail,
an imprint of Profile Books Ltd
3A Exmouth House
Pine Street
London EC1R 0JH
www.serpentstail.com

ISBN 978-1852425364

Printed and bound in Italy by LEGO SpA
Designed by Sue Lamble sue@lambledesign.demon.co.uk

Set in 9pt Palatino

10 9 8 7 6 5 4 3 2

Contents

Preface
Marina Warner

IN THE SEVENTEENTH CENTURY in Rome, visitors on the Grand Tour sought out the museum that the polymath Athanasius Kircher had assembled, a *wunderkammer* of antiquities – memorials, figurines, amulets – and of natural phenomena – fossils, curious insects, mandrake roots. Kircher was a man of prodigiously far-ranging interests, a magus, a scientist, a writer, a theologian, an astronomer, an alchemist, and a Jesuit who collected the marvels of god's creation but also found the divine signature inscribed, as he put it, in the handiwork of all his creatures, pagan and Christian. His cabinet of wonders founded the idea of a personal museum that expresses individual desire. Sigmund Freud is, in many ways, a fitting successor, and his house maps the mind of a man as well as the mind of an age.

The first time I visited the Freud Museum, I was astonished that Freud's rooms, including his study, had been preserved apparently untouched for over half a century: time had been stilled by Anna Freud when she did not move any of her father's things, not even his spectacles on the desk. Her filial piety struck me as overwhelming, self-effacing, and very poignant (she can be overheard on the home movie about Freud's last birthday saying, 'That's me in the background.'). But my feelings have changed, and I no longer see Anna Freud's dedication as self-sacrificing. For she was not simply worshipping the idol of her father in Oedipal fashion; she was acknowledging the importance of his thought, and through this tribute, placing her work in his lineage, claiming respect for her contribution as well as that of her colleagues. Her act of enshrinement draws attention to Freud as an event in history, a new geography of the mind, not only a person. She was also commemorating an intellectual world that, in 1939, was being destroyed. Freud's unique gifts of inquiry, learning and imagination saturate the images, books, sculptures, gems and furniture, but the museum also brings vividly before one's eyes the culture that nurtured thinkers like him and like Anna, and that the war against Nazi Germany, in its most idealistic avowed intentions, was fought to save and perpetuate.

Because Freud worked at home, both in Vienna and in this last refuge in Hampstead, and Anna followed this example, the house also makes another point: it reveals, in psychoanalytic fashion, how interwoven the mind is, how fantasy flickers through the ordinary fabric of daily life and its mundane routine. Freud surrounded himself with artefacts of great beauty and value, but they were also tools of thought, the kitchen utensils of his imagination. His objects that took on a life beyond art and metaphor in his thought and became central to his analysis of mind: he did not simply look at images but worked with the ideas embodied by Athena the Goddess of Wisdom, Eros the God of Love, Oedipus interrogating the Sphinx and discovering her riddle, and by numerous funerary effigies associated with the fear of death. The poet HD famously recalled in her memoir that Freud, showing her one of his favourite statuettes of Athena, remarked that she was perfect, except that she had lost her spear. His Erotes lift their tunics to reveal their genitals with impish delight: they embody the principle of eros, that Freud has so deeply naturalized in twentieth-century thinking that we cannot really consider human sexuality without it. Oedipus is the protagonist of his most famous theory, of course, but he is also a kind of self-portrait, a questor who is disturbed to the roots of his being by the secrets he desires to uncover.

Freud's house also conveys the interconnectedness of his work with his family, friends, visitors and patients or analysands; it communicates how the 'talking cure' that gave such vital expression to people's inner lives developed in conditions of reciprocal exchange with one another; those loves, friendships, alliances are webbed into the very walls and rooms of his home. The absent presences that once lay on the famous couch are not Freud's: its emptiness, draped in that flying carpet for unconscious voyaging, is crowded with the ghosts of those who talked to him, gave him the stories about desire and trauma and phobia and fixation and neurosis and all those words and conditions that have become a part of our vocabulary and passed into our consciousness.

Museums that keep alive the working conditions of an artist are not very common in England. France, with its heightened sense of *le patrimoine*, is richer in this kind of memorial: Montaigne's tower, George Sand's country retreat, Gustave Moreau's studio house in Paris reveal their owners; but they are shrines, hushed by the past and filled with relics. Brancusi's studio, left to the state by the artist, was moved to the parvis of the Pompidou Centre, and has recently been redecorated, within a modernist white cube and under glass: the effect is an inert diorama, a waxwork.

By contrast, the Freud Museum is a vibrantly living organism. It is a fascinating cult site, a place of mythic memory, a shrine, a monument, a haunted house. But it also continues to pulse to a lively current of problems and challenges. Sigmund Freud shaped the twentieth century idea of what a person is; we would not recognize ourselves without him; his influence reverberates in Henry James and Virginia Woolf, Alfred Hitchcock and David Lynch, the art of the Surrealists and the lure of advertisements.

Freud's stories have become our stories, his map our map, his questions our questions, and the Freud Museum, through its collections, its lively programme of study and lectures and its imaginative contemporary art commissions, continues to invigorate the tradition with yet more stories, questions, ideas, from which we still take our bearings.

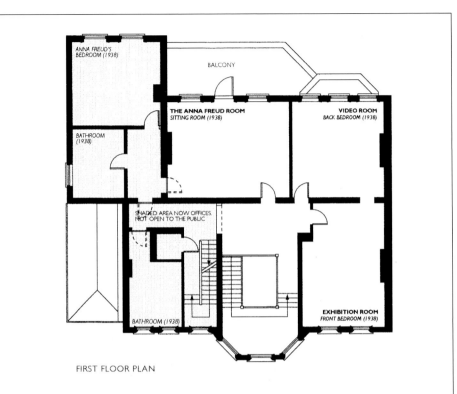

ANNA FREUD'S
BEDROOM (1938)

BALCONY

THE ANNA FREUD ROOM
SITTING ROOM (1938)

VIDEO ROOM
BACK BEDROOM (1938)

BATHROOM
(1938)

SHADED AREA NOW OFFICES.
NOT OPEN TO THE PUBLIC

BATHROOM (1938)

EXHIBITION ROOM
FRONT BEDROOM (1938)

FIRST FLOOR PLAN

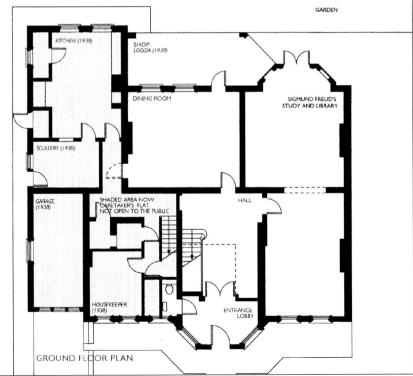

GARDEN

KITCHEN (1938)

SHOP
LOGGIA (1938)

DINING ROOM

SIGMUND FREUD'S
STUDY AND LIBRARY

SCULLERY (1938)

GARAGE
(1938)

SHADED AREA NOW
CARETAKER'S FLAT.
NOT OPEN TO THE PUBLIC

HALL

HOUSEKEEPER
(1938)

ENTRANCE
LOBBY

GROUND FLOOR PLAN

Introduction

'20 MARESFIELD GARDENS as I hope our last address on this planet,
but not to be used before the end of September. Our ~~united~~ own
house!… And far too beautiful for us…' Sigmund Freud wrote on
22 August, 1938. In June, after months of nerve-wracking turmoil
in Nazi Vienna, Freud and his family had finally managed to flee
Austria. They were glad to escape with their lives. It was an unex-
pected blessing that virtually all their possessions could be sent
after them. These included Freud's prized collection of antiquities. 'All the Egyptians, the Chinese and the Greek women have
arrived, have stood up to the journey with little damage, and look

much more impressive here than in Berggasse,' he wrote on 8 October, just after they had moved in. With the arrival of his antiquities Freud's new home was complete. This large brick house with its well-proportioned rooms was a haven for the last year of his life. Here he was able to practise psychoanalysis, write his final manuscripts, receive visitors and continue correspondence until the last weeks of his life.

The heart of the house was, and is, Freud's study and consulting room. Here his antiquities' collection and library were set

A corner of the study with showcases of Greek vases and Egyptian antiquities

up for him much as they had been in Vienna. The room represents a fragment of the complex intellectual life of *fin de siècle* Vienna transported to London. Colourful oriental rugs cover the floor, tables and the psychoanalytic couch. The walls are lined with bookshelves dismantled and moved from Berggasse 19. The books reflect Freud's professional studies – neurology, psychology, psychoanalysis – and also his intense interest in archaeology, ancient history and anthropology. The collection of antiquities fills the glass cases between the bookshelves. The contents of these books and cabinets are among the varied raw materials which Freud's intellect and imagination combined and transmuted into the basis of psychoanalysis.

A museum dedicated to the founder of psychoanalysis cannot be a static shrine. Museums imply order and visibility, but Freud overturned the hierarchy of what was felt to be important and unimportant. The raw materials of psychoanalysis are fleeting and invisible – associations of ideas, dreams, slips of the tongue or even silence. Apparent stability conceals strife and disorder. The letter quoted at the beginning of this introduction offers an example of the tension between an ordered surface and the play of emotions. 'I hope' has been added in the margin, and it reminds us of the anxiety of the refugee: the crossed-out 'united' may reveal a vain hope of harmony. That lost or marginalised hope might refer to the psychoanalytical movement, which was at the time seething with disagreements (and still is). Disagreement surrounded Freud's last published work as well. *Moses and Monotheism* was to release a storm of criticism that has still not died down. A man who disturbed the sleep of the world could not be expected to leave a legacy of peace. The museum's apparent calm is the residue of one man's lifetime's struggle. And his words to the BBC in 1938 still apply, perhaps now more than ever: 'the struggle is not yet over.'

The emergence of the museum itself, however, was a natural development. After Freud's death in 1939, his wife Martha made no changes to the study during the rest of her life and Anna Freud, the youngest of the Freuds' six children, subsequently kept it just as it was in her father's lifetime. She herself lived and practised psychoanalysis at 20 Maresfield Gardens for over forty years and gained a high reputation in her own right as the founder of child psychoanalysis.

Two years before her death in 1982 she sold the land and buildings at 20 Maresfield Gardens to a registered English charity. This purchase was made possible by the generosity of Muriel Gardiner, a longtime friend of the Freud family, through her New-Land Foundation. In her will Anna Freud bequeathed the contents of the house to the charity to become a museum dedicated to her father's life and work. The Museum opened in 1986. It was first managed by a committee in London and through a joint committee in New York, whose members were drawn from Sigmund

Freud Archives Inc. and from the New-Land Foundation. Since 2006 it has been a British charitable limited company governed by a London Board of Trustees. The Freud Museum commemorates the work of both Sigmund and Anna Freud through its publications, its education programme and international exhibitions. It aims to preserve their extraordinary working environment and also to serve as an international centre of Freud studies and information, both for scholars and the general public.

Nowadays it is hardly possible to think of the mind or of mental properties without invoking Freudian categories; indeed, entire libraries could be filled with works on the subject. This guidebook sketches some aspects of Freud's life and work, but it cannot claim to be a general introduction to psychoanalysis or a rounded biographical portrait. It aims instead to present Sigmund Freud and his world indirectly through his house and possessions. For this reason, the book follows the ground plan of the museum room by room. Each space offers the visitor a series of glimpses of the man and his world.

Freud's intellectual revolution was summarized in the phrase: 'the ego is not master in its own house.' [S.E. XVII:143] * At one level this guidebook simply offers a tour of an actual house. But its exhibits are also aspects of that metaphorical house, the human mind. Some of them are artefacts created by vanished cultures whose world and intentions are often hardly intelligible; others are recent books and images that speak to or for the twentieth century. The question of what place Freud's work will occupy in the next century has yet to be answered. A model of thought processes, whether correct or mistaken, can never be irrelevant to the way we imagine ourselves.

*Note on references

Quotations from Freud's published works are followed by the abbreviation S.E. with volume and page number. This refers to the authoritative edition of his writings: *The Standard Edition of the Complete Psychological Works of Sigmund Freud* (translated from the German under the General Editorship of James Strachey). London: The Hogarth Press, 1953–1974.

Quotations from letters are derived from a wide range of published and unpublished sources and no source reference is given in the text. However, some of the basic sources are listed in a bibliography at the end of the book (*see* **Further Reading** p. 127).

The house

IN SPRING 1938 THE SEARCH for a suitable house for Freud's household of five was entrusted to Ernst, the Freuds' youngest son, an architect, who had emigrated to London in 1933. To be able to rely on Ernst to find accommodation, both temporary and permanent, must have eased the burdens that their traumatic upheaval imposed on the family. On their arrival in June they were able to move straight into a rented house at 39 Elsworthy Road, but it was free only until September. Freud wrote to his brother Alexander in July 1938: 'The next and most difficult problem is to find a house that corresponds at one and the same time to our complicated demands and to our modest means.' The search was not to be too protracted. Later that month Freud noted in his diary: 'House purchase concluded.' At this point he had not even seen the house.

Freud's architect son Ernst, with his wife Lucie. In 1938 he found and converted the house at 20 Maresfield Gardens for his father

The price was £6,500. Barclays Bank provided a £4000 loan (which was not redeemed until 1943). In September he was legally registered as owner at the Land Registry and at the end of the month he and his family moved into 20 Maresfield Gardens.

As visitors walk up Maresfield Gardens away from the noise and bustle of the Finchley Road, a quieter world envelops them. The street rises in a gentle slope to the north and on either side are lofty houses, most of them constructed around the turn of the century. They display a variety of styles, some detached, others semi-detached, but they are all substantial, two stories high with basements and attics. Their size and their decorative embellishments, such as stained-glass windows, indicate that they were intended to be houses of some pretension. Many are now divided into flats, some were replaced in the 1960s, while numbers 12, 14 and 21 house the Anna Freud Centre.

As London rapidly expanded throughout the second half of the nineteenth century, the area surrounding Maresfield Gardens was the scene of energetic building activity. So it was unusual that a sizeable parcel of land on the east side of the road remained undeveloped. In the nineteenth century it formed part of the estate of the Maryon-Wilson family who possessed large tracts of Hampstead, including Hampstead Heath. Maresfield Gardens was named after the village of Maresfield in Sussex, and nearby roads are also named after places in Sussex. In 1884 John Hill purchased the land that now encompasses numbers 18, 20 and 22, probably with the intention of building three dwellings. His plans must have been interrupted since nothing was built on the site until around 1920. The builder was James Tomblin who employed Albert Hastilow to make the plans for the house.

Five years before Freud bought the house the auctioneers Goldschmidt and Howland produced a brochure containing an enthusiastic description of 20 Maresfield Gardens: 'A very fine and well planned modern freehold residence… enjoying a delightful sunny aspect with splendidly proportioned lofty rooms and in excellent condition throughout.'

Prospective purchasers could view its eight bedrooms, three reception rooms, three bathrooms and two garages. The brochure was at pains to point out that the domestic offices were not in a basement, an agreeable feature which distinguished it from many of the older houses in the street, and it is clear that there was sufficient accommodation for a live-in servant. To make this fine residence complete there were gardens at the front and back of the house, and even a tennis lawn at the rear. The estate agents were also keen to emphasise that at least three of the rooms could accommodate a billiards table – not a likely object on the Freuds' list of priorities! This was a substantial, impressive property conveniently placed for transport – a fine residence for a prosperous middle-class family.

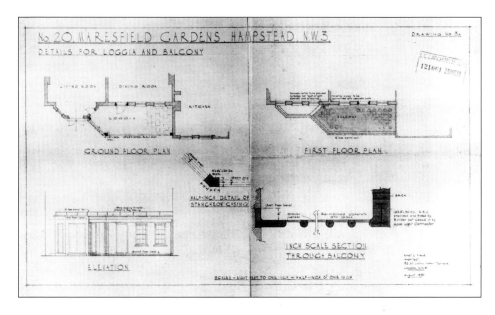

Ernst Freud's plans for the loggia and balcony to be added to the rear of the house

Despite boasting the most up-to-date modern conveniences for its time (gas, electric light and power, telephone, a constant hot water installation, partial system of central heating), the house was built in brick in a revivalist style looking back to the architecture of Queen Anne in the early eighteenth century. This style was highly fashionable in Hampstead during the 1920s and '30s, and can be seen throughout Hampstead Garden Suburb. Ernst Freud, a modernist, described it as 'neo-Georgian'. Freud's letters of the time reveal his obvious delight with the house. 'Our own home. It is very beautiful… Light, comfortable spacious…' His enthusiasm is quite infectious: 'Our new house was originally beautifully built and has been splendidly renovated by Ernst. We have it incomparably better than at Berggasse and even than Grinzing. "From poverty to white bread" as the proverb says.' Renovations continued throughout August and September of 1938. With wry amusement Freud described his son's alterations: '…Ernst who has transformed the house into a ruin in order to restore it anew in a more suitable state for us. He is building in a lift, making two rooms into one or the other way around, sheer sorcery translated into architectural terms.' Ernst, with his modernist's sensibility, removed some of the more extraneous decorative features such as the dado rail. He knocked two ground floor rooms into one to create a combined consulting room, library, study and sitting room. At one end, French windows opened into the garden, one of the great delights of the house for Freud who loved flowers. Ernst's major piece of construction was an open-sided loggia (which has now been glazed and houses the shop). The roof is glazed with thick round glass, forming a terrace for the room above, and providing a sheltered space in the garden.

The winter of 1938 revealed some of the design faults of British buildings. The sash windows which allow so much light into a room, also allow cold air to penetrate. Freud was not impressed: 'It is bitterly cold, the plumbing has frozen up and British deficiencies in overcoming the heating problem are clearly evident.' (The sash windows still allow drafts of cold air to penetrate.) As spring returned, the garden could once more be enjoyed, and Ernest Jones wrote that Freud took particular delight in the almond tree in the front garden. The weather in May 1939 was fine enough for Freud's last birthday, his eighty-third, to be celebrated in the garden. Family, friends and dogs gathered and, resuming the family tradition, a birthday table covered with gifts and flowers was set up under Ernst's loggia.

As Freud's health dwindled and his life moved inexorably to its final stage, his existence was confined to his study where a bed was set up for him. Here, on 23 September 1939, he died.

Freud in England

FREUD FIRST CAME TO England in 1875, as a nineteen-year-old student, to visit his relatives in Manchester. Darwin was still alive and Disraeli was Prime Minister. After his return home to Vienna he wrote to his friend Eduard Silberstein: '... I would rather live there than here, in spite of fog and rain, drunkenness and conservatism. Many peculiarities of the English character and country

On Monday 6 June 1938 the *Daily Herald* reported Freud's arrival in England. The photo shows him en route in Paris, escorted by the psychoanalyst Princess Marie Bonaparte. The inset photo shows his first and temporary accommodation in London, at 39 Elsworthy Road, next to Primrose Hill

which other continentals would find intolerable fit in very well with my nature...'

But it was not until June 1938 that Freud finally came to live in England. As he wrote to his son Ernst on 12 May that year: 'Two prospects keep me going in these grim times: to rejoin you all and – to die in freedom.' He arrived on a German Nazi passport because Austria, his homeland, had just disappeared as a nation after the German Anschluss on 11 March 1938. Thus he became an 'enemy alien' at the outbreak of war. But that was not for want of a campaign to get him British citizenship. One of the members of that campaign was H.G. Wells. On 14 July 1939 he wrote to Freud saying: '... a number of us want you to do us that honour [of becoming a British citizen].' Freud's response was enthusiastic. He replied immediately: 'Indeed, you cannot have known that since I first came over to England as a boy of eighteen years [actually he was nineteen], it became an intense wish phantasy of mine to settle in this country and become an Englishman. Two of my half-brothers had done so fifteen years before.' At first it looks as if he is saying that this intense phantasy to be an Englishman started when he first came to England as a young man. But having said that his half-brothers had arrived in England fifteen years earlier – that is, when he was three years old – Freud adds: 'But an infantile phantasy needs a bit of examination before it can be admitted to reality.'

The initial phantasy of becoming English was therefore not produced by the well-educated young man, who had read Dickens, spoke excellent English, and liked what he had seen of English culture: it was the dream of the three-year-old child who wanted to carry on playing with the companions who had been taken away from him when his father took the family to Vienna.

In the perspective of this wish to be English, the whole of Freud's life takes on a kind of symmetry. It begins in a little paradise amid the fields and woods of Moravia, among a large family and relations, with playmates of his own age. Then comes the fall from grace. The family splits up. The older half-brothers and their children leave for the mythical country of England: Freud's parents take him and his sister to Vienna. What follows are years of poverty and struggle in a crowded and unwelcoming city. These first unfavourable memories obviously set the tone for the rest of his life there. Vienna is a sort of purgatory he has to work through and battle against, it is a trial that has been imposed upon him by

his father. It is where he must prove himself a man against all the odds – opposition, ignorance and antisemitism. Meanwhile, in the back of his mind there remains that fantasy of England, a friendly place where things are better, where his favourite playmate has gone, where all the family can be together again.

The town where Freud was born, Freiberg in Moravia (now Příbor in the Czech Republic)

And finally there was the eleventh-hour escape from Nazi Austria. The reception from the British press made him realize for the first time what it was to be famous. And he loved their bright new house with its garden, so unlike the dark apartment in Berggasse. His extended family were all close together again, they were safe, they were living in beautiful surroundings. In short, it was as if he had returned to his idealized origins; it was almost like the lost paradise of Freiberg regained. But paradise remains a myth or mirage. As he wrote to Ernst Simmel on 26 June 1938, 'the hideous news from Vienna and inevitable sympathy with the fate of so many others who are having a bad time cast a dark shadow over our happiness'.

Once settled in England Freud could at last return to the work that had been interrupted by the Anschluss. The first task was to complete *Moses and Monotheism*; he did so within six weeks of his arrival. Almost immediately afterwards he embarked on what was to be a summary of psychoanalysis. This work was interrupted by a recurrence of the cancer that led to his last serious operation. It was published in note form after his death as *An Outline of Psycho-Analysis*.

During the final years in Vienna Freud had greatly reduced his psychoanalytical practice and in London he found himself at first with no patients. Eventually, however, he took on four regular patients and continued treating them until ill-health forced him to give up his practice at the beginning of August 1939. There were also colleagues who came for analysis or 'after-analyses', such as Ruth Mack Brunswick, a loyal friend since the twenties. She left for the United States a few weeks before Freud died. Freud also gave Dorothy Burlingham ninety-nine sessions of training analysis over six months from the time of his arrival in England, and brief analyses to other visiting analysts, such as Smiley Blanton.

Freud was of course a patient himself. Max Schur, a close friend, whom Freud referred to as his 'personal physician', spent as much time as he possibly could with Freud in London, leaving his patient reluctantly while making urgent arrangements for his own family to reach safety in America.

Freud had always been sociable and a small blue leather notebook lists many of the visitors who came to see him in England. Several of the visitors Freud noted are specialists whose advice was sought in connection with his cancer and its radium treatment. Others are mentioned in his so-called 'Brief Chronicle' or note diary for 1929 to 1939. Some went unrecorded and these tended to be regular callers, such as Ernest Jones. The roll-call of Freud's London visitors reflects all aspects of his family and professional life, as well as his personal interests and his preoccupations at that time. It also testifies to his wide reputation and to the great variety of individuals prominent in their own fields whose work had felt the impact of psychoanalysis. There were numerous visits from colleagues who had worked closely with Freud for years, such as Max Eitingon or Jeanne Lampl-de Groot, and from members of the British Psycho-Analytical Society, such as Barbara Low, Roger Money-Kyrle, Edward Glover, Walter Schmiedeberg, Joan Riviere and Melanie Klein, whose pioneering and influential work on child analysis was at odds with Anna Freud's.

The move to London made possible several reunions with family members. Among those who visited were Sam Freud, the

Freud at work in the study at Maresfield Gardens

nephew from Manchester, whom Freud had not seen since his last visit to London in 1908. Eva, a favourite grandchild of Freud and Martha, came for her last visit in August 1939. Other relatives to appear were the grandson Ernstl, who had escaped via Paris with the help of Marie Bonaparte. His intention had been to join his father, Max Halberstadt, in South Africa, but he decided to stay in England instead. Freud's brother Alexander and his wife lived not far away in Hove while waiting for a visa to allow them to rejoin their son, Harry, in Canada.

Princess Marie Bonaparte, who was by now almost a member of the family, visited nine times, often with gifts of antiquities from Paris, such as the bronze Venus that Freud mentioned in his diary on 16 October 1938. Marie Bonaparte remained indefatigable, trying in vain to bring Freud's sisters to safety in France and bringing medical experts to see Freud, for example Professor Lacassagne of the Institut Marie Curie in Paris.

Despite Freud's debilitating illness, many of his visitors came to discuss particular work matters. Hanns Sachs, Freud's longtime

Freud, Professor Lacassagne, Princess Marie Bonaparte and Freud's eldest daughter Mathilde by the loggia in early 1939

colleague and champion, came over from Boston in July 1939. (He had prudently left Berlin as early as 1932.) He called on Freud daily, discussing with Freud his plans for starting up *Imago* again as an English-language journal devoted to applied psychoanalysis. There were other publishing projects to be attended to. Stanley Unwin of Allen and Unwin, interested in publishing Freud's complete works, visited.

Moses and Monotheism and its publication were discussed during several of the visits. Charles Singer, an eminent historian of science, came twice, suggesting politely that Freud should keep that work in his desk, as did also the Jewish Biblical scholar Abraham Yahuda, whose name heads Freud's list of visitors. But Freud was undeterred. His main concern was to expedite the work's publication. Leonard and Virginia Woolf of the Hogarth

Press came for tea. In his autobiography Leonard Woolf wrote that Freud was 'not only a genius, but also, unlike many geniuses, an extraordinarily nice man'. The meeting '...was not an easy interview. He was extraordinarily courteous in an old-fashioned way – for instance, almost ceremoniously, he presented Virginia with a flower. There was something about him as of a half-extinct volcano, something sombre, suppressed, reserved. He gave me a feeling of great gentleness, great strength.' When Leonard Woolf suggested that the word 'Monotheism' be dropped from the book's title since it might frighten off the English public, Freud not only indignantly refused but wrote to his American publisher, Blanche Knopf, insisting that she too must stick to the original title.

Among the visitors, H.G. Wells, one of the few British literary figures Freud had known previously, declared himself sympathetic to Freud's *Moses* book, finding its suggestions 'immensely probable'. Many other literary and artistic figures came to pay their respects. The novelist Arnold Zweig came to England to be near Freud, writing after he had left to express concern that his visits had sapped Freud's reserves of strength. Stefan Zweig, an internationally famous writer, came too, bringing Salvador Dali to meet his hero. Freud was surprised to find himself impressed by Dali, writing to Zweig the following day: '...I have been inclined to regard the surrealists, who apparently have adopted me as their patron saint, as complete fools ...That young Spaniard, with his candid fanatical eyes and his undeniable technical mastery, has changed my estimate.'

Dali sketched Freud during the visit, and the resulting drawing now hangs on the first floor landing. Freud also sat for the sculptor Willy Lévy and the photographer Marcel Sternberger while at Maresfield Gardens, and the BBC came to make a recording as he worked at his desk. Other representatives of the arts who visited were the celebrated French singer, Yvette Guilbert, a living link to Freud's days in Paris, and Engel Lund, an acquaintance of Anna Freud's, who gave a recital of Icelandic and Jewish folksongs. On the day of the recital, the beloved chow Lun was finally released from six months' quarantine, and Freud's thoughts and conversation were primarily about her on this occasion.

When Arthur Koestler came to visit he asked Freud to write an article for the German émigré weekly in Paris that he edited. Freud responded with a short piece on anti-semitism, his first work to be published from exile. Others arrived to see Freud with the political and social situation of the Jews in mind, among them the famous Zionist leader Chaim Weizmann, whom Freud respected, the Jewish campaigner Norman Bentwich, the anti-Nazi Prince Loewenstein, and Margaret Lady Stonborough, Wittgenstein's sister, who had left Vienna in protest against the Nazis, although herself in no personal danger at the time.

The Royal Society Charter Book brought to Freud for his signature on 23 June 1938

Other visitors were less immediately concerned with the worsening political situation. Among them were Meena Gunn, who had received some analytic training in Vienna, bringing Freud an Egyptian antiquity, the writer Rahel Bardi, anthropologist Bronislaw Malinowski and the joint Nobel prize-winners for their work on the chemical transmission of nerve impulses, Otto Loewi and Henry Hallett Dale. Also among the early visitors were three representatives of the Royal Society which had honoured Freud with Foreign Membership in 1936; they had broken with the Society's tradition by bringing the Charter Book to be signed at his home, a privilege previously afforded only to the king. Freud's signature shared the book with those of Newton and his scientific hero, Darwin.

The pleasure of these visits was set against Freud's health and the world situation, both worsening in parallel. Meetings with family members and old friends increasingly took on an air of final farewell. The diary notes for August 1939 record a series of leave-takings. One of his final letters, written to the poet Albrecht Schaeffer on 19 August, ends with the words: '...I really have nothing else to do but follow the advice of your verses: To wait and wait.'

The hall, landing and dining room

LIGHT FROM THE HIGH WINDOWS above the stairwell fills the hall and creates a sense of space and freedom. The Freuds had lived for forty-seven years in a dark apartment in Vienna and the airiness of the house at Maresfield Gardens impressed them. 'It is very beautiful... Light, comfortable, spacious,' Freud wrote on 8 October 1938 to Jeanne Lampl-de Groot. On 3 November he wrote to Max Eitingon: 'We have it incomparably better than at Berggasse...'

Opposite the stairs, in the hall, hangs a painting of a flight of stairs leading up to the Villa d'Este at Tivoli near Rome. The observer of this picture, about to climb the stairs to the next storey of the museum, is drawn into the painting, as if mounting those stairs up to the villa. This was a view Freud would first have seen in 1901. For many years before that he had felt the lure of the Mediterranean and its culture and had longed to travel to Rome. But some neurotic hindrance had held him back. When he eventually arrived there for the first time he was delighted by the city and the reality of its wonders. It was from an excursion to Tivoli on 8 September 1901 that he wrote home: 'Everything is real, hill, olive grove, cypresses, deep blue sky, figs, peaches and dark brown people.' Three years later, during his only visit to Athens, he was to experience a similar surprise at the reality of the Acropolis.

The longing to travel, Freud felt, is linked to the desire to escape from the pressures of family life 'like the force which drives so many adolescent children to run away from home'. Part of its pleasure lies in the fulfilment of early wishes, and is rooted in early dissatisfactions. 'When first one catches sight of the sea, crosses the ocean and experiences as realities cities and lands which for so long had been distant, unattainable things of desire – one feels oneself like a hero who has performed deeds of improbable greatness.' [SE XXII.247]

Freud's flight to England in 1938 was his last actual journey. Though no pleasure, it was certainly heroic in its way. And after his arrival, on 13 June, Freud experienced yet again a sense of 'unreality' and wrote to Jeanne Lampl-de Groot: '…everything is still uncustomary and as if unreal, a clear sense of alienation.' Once in London his age and sickness meant he could now only travel in his imagination. Indeed, he may not even have set foot on this landing because his heart was too weak to allow him to walk upstairs. When the house had been converted his son Ernst had had a lift installed to take him up to his bedroom on the first floor.

Freud's wife Martha is remembered sitting at the window

The Villa d'Este, Tivoli, painted in 1893 by Ludwig Hans Fischer

on the landing where she could see people coming and going. Her sister Minna Bernays would sometimes join her, though she was often ill and her sight was poor. (She died in 1942.) The two women were Freud's life-long companions and their characters were complementary. Martha was a gracious and efficient manager

Freud and Martha on the loggia, 1939

of the household. After his death, on 5 November 1939, she summarized the role she had fulfilled in a letter to Paul Federn: 'I have been granted more than a lifetime in which I have been allowed to look after him, to shield him from the troubles of everyday life.' The children remembered their aunt Minna as less approachable, a woman of intelligence and capable of cutting remarks. As far as Freud's wants and needs were concerned, Martha's love and protection were vital. It would

Minna Bernays, Freud's sister-in-law

be hard to imagine his life or work without that basis. Her constant love, like that of his mother, was part of the hidden foundation of his confidence.

Minna's presence and contribution to the household is less easily defined. In 1895 she had moved into Berggasse 'for a few months' and stayed for good. During the earlier years of Freud's marriage, when Martha was fully occupied with the children, Minna was an intellectual companion and even accompanied Freud occasionally on holidays. Her health was never as good as her sister's and she often went on cures to Meran; this also restricted her contribution to the running of the household.

In Vienna, Martha Freud had done all the shopping herself and she continued that habit when they arrived in England, although she was now seventy-seven years old. Of the old people, she was the one who adapted fastest to life in England. Self-effacing as she was, her qualities are not always appreciated, but her surviving letters reveal a warm and intelligent personality. Initially only Freud's side of their engagement correspondence from 1882 to 1886 was published and this left readers with the impression of her only as the mute object of his passionate love. The long-awaited publication of her side of the correspondence brings her back to life. On 6 October 1883 he wrote to her: 'You write so intelligently and to the point that I am just a little afraid of you. I think it all goes to show once more how quickly women outdistance men.' Though Martha will always be seen through the prism of her relationship to her husband, it is at the very least worth bearing in mind how immense his debt was to her throughout their long marriage.

The books now in the shelves on the landing were Anna Freud's. They include some unusual works of especial significance to her, such as the poems of Herbert Davy Jones, some of which she translated into German during her twenties. Herbert Davy Jones married Ernest Jones's ex-companion, Loe Kann, who was a patient of Freud's and a friend to him and Anna – one of several lively and intelligent women who were protective friends for Anna in her youth. Another, whose books are here, was Lou Andreas-Salomé. We also find Princess Marie Bonaparte's book on her chow Topsy, in the German translation which Anna and Sigmund Freud did together in 1937-38. And the lighter side of Anna's reading is evident here in escapist literature such as the Scarlet Pimpernel stories of Baroness Orczy.

As you enter the museum a print of Moses with the Tablets of the Law confronts you across the entrance hall. It is from an engraving by Krüger, done in 1770, after Rembrandt's original of 1659, and it serves as a reminder of Freud's long-standing fascination with the figure of Moses.

Moses

Other Moses images can be found in the collection and archives: these include a print of Michelangelo's statue of Moses in the church of San Pietro in Vincoli, Rome, and also a sketch made of that statue when Freud was studying it 'for three lonely weeks' in 1912. In Freud's guidebook to Rome, he underlined the explanation of the statue's posture as one of restrained wrath at the faithless mob 'which rejoices when it has regained its illusory idols'. He wrote this phrase in 1914 in his paper 'The Moses of Michelangelo', published anonymously, partly because it was non-analytical, but perhaps more significantly because it gave indirect vent to Freud's own wrath against such faithless followers of his as Jung.

In 1934 Freud returned to the figure of Moses, but this time it was anti-semitism which goaded him. On 30th September he wrote to Arnold Zweig: 'Faced by the renewed persecutions, one asks oneself again how the Jew came to be what he is and why he has drawn upon himself this undying hatred. I soon found the formula: Moses created the Jew. And my essay received the title: *The Man Moses, a Historical Novel.*'

Over the following years he added two further chapters to the work and published it under the title *Moses and Monotheism.* One of the messages of this 'historical novel' is that history is written, or etched in our hearts and minds, as dangerous wishes hidden in self-protective fictions; as condensations of disparate figures over time; as displacements of threatening ideas to more comfortable ones. These transformations resemble that 'secondary revision' which reworks our instinctual urges into dream imagery. For Freud what we call 'history' is written like a dream.

Freud's hypothesis that Moses was not a Jew, but an Egyptian aristocrat, was founded on hotly disputed Biblical scholarship and his radical concepts of the *real event* and the *return of the repressed* infuriated Jews and Christians alike. Many implored him not to publish, among them Charles Singer to whom he wrote on 31 October 1938:

> 'I have spent my whole life standing up for what I have considered to be the scientific truth, even when it was uncomfortable and unpleasant for my fellow men. I cannot end up with an act of disavowal. Your letter contains the assurance that testifies to your intelligence, that everything I write is bound to cause misunderstanding and – may I add – indignation. Well, we Jews have been reproached for growing cowardly in the course of the centuries. (Once upon a time we were a valiant nation.) In this transformation I had no share. So I must risk it.'

If Freud identified with Moses, it was with the circumstances of his situation rather than with the figure. Freud himself had brought a (scientific) law to his followers, but if it was truly scientific then it was at odds with faith and dogma. He repeatedly asserted that the basic concepts of science could not be written in tablets of stone. In both the Krüger print and the Michelangelo statue it is unclear whether Moses is grasping the tablets of the law as a prelude to smashing them or whether he is presenting them to the people.

After finishing the *Moses* book Freud wrote two unfinished 'primers' – *An Outline of Psychoanalysis* and *Some Elementary Lessons in Psychoanalysis*. Having created the culture and tradition of psychoanalysis, Freud wanted them preserved after his death. But he too had to balance doctrine against iconoclasm. The basic principles of the subject had to be retained while at the same time flexibility and growth needed to be encouraged. Freud had founded a tradition that could survive only if it remained undogmatic. Its laws are 'in the nature of conventions'.

Furniture

Biedermeier table on the landing

Generations of the Freud family are represented by the furniture now in the Museum. Their tastes and journeyings through time and place are reflected in a rich variety of styles. The Austrian painted furniture belonged to Anna Freud and Dorothy Burlingham and was part of the furnishings of their country

Nineteenth-century painted cupboard

retreat at Hochrotherd near Vienna. Simple in design, the cupboards and chests were decorated in the eighteenth century to simulate more refined and expensive veneered furniture. This style is best exemplified by a large cupboard in the dining room, dated 1744. By the nineteenth century designs were more fanciful and purely decorative and were sometimes embellished with poetry, like the cupboard in the video room with its couplets celebrating a marriage. The unsophisticated rhymes twice feature the word 'joy' (*Freude*), which must have amused and attracted the Freuds.

Intricate marquetry and simplicity of design are the hallmarks of the Biedermeier furniture which is well represented in the collection, and was one of the most distinctive features of the Freud family apartment at Berggasse 19. Much of it neo-classical, it reflects the taste of the prosperous bourgeoisie in the late eighteenth and early nineteenth century in Austria and the German states. Most of the Biedermeier furniture now at Maresfield Gardens would have been made at least one or two generations earlier than the 1880s when Sigmund and Martha Freud were setting up their home. It may have belonged to Martha's family, the Bernays, who were rather more prosperous than the Freud family, or been purchased by Sigmund and Martha when there was a renewal of interest in the style in the 1890s.

Anna Freud's taste was by no means limited to the antique. Her own rooms included furniture made by modernists, one of whom was Felix Augenfeld, an architect and friend of her brother Ernst, and the designer of Freud's armchair. She also had chairs designed by Mies van der Rohe and tables by Alvar Aalto.

The sheltered domestic world created by the women of the Freud family did not cease to develop with emigration. They acquired a refectory table in England and the comfortable chairs placed invitingly on the landing are English in manufacture. They represent the Freud family's assimilation into its new environment.

Alpine souvenir pictures

Entering the dining room, you notice a composite set of alpine pictures to the right of the door. This curious souvenir of the Austrian spa town of Bad Gastein and its surrounding countryside relates to the weeks Freud spent there, first in 1916 and then every summer from 1919 to 1923, taking the waters for his chronic digestive problems. Visitors with a knowledge of Freud's biography frequently conclude that the 'Bellevue' depicted in the top left hand corner must be the hotel near Vienna where Freud had his famous 'Irma dream'. This was the first dream he analyzed to his own satisfaction. On 12 June 1900, after the publication of *The Interpretation of Dreams*, he wrote to his friend Wilhelm Fliess: 'Do you think that one day the house will bear a marble tablet with the words: *In this house on July 24, 1895, the secret of dreams was revealed to Dr. Sigmund Freud*.'

But the inset picture entitled 'Bellevue' is another, less famous Bellevue, near Bad Gastein. Nevertheless, the coincidence of names is itself dreamlike: it superimposes one set of associations upon another.

The symbolic equation which most often structures our perception of countryside is that of the landscape and the human

body. In this light, the Alpine picture, with its mountains, valleys, waterfalls and church towers is replete with male and female sexual symbols. But it is not reducible to them alone. The metaphor of the body is more complicated and male and female elements are combined.

The mountain scenery in this picture poses a general question about landscapes and Freud. Do they have a more direct relation to his creativity than we might have supposed? For Freud, his holidays in the country were not only relaxation but also a time when he could settle down to creative work. When he contacted the warring forces within himself, in a sense he was placing himself in a landscape which was a 'primal scene' imbued with the procreative capacities of a combined male and female parent figure.

When we look at the landscapes of Da Vinci's high art or when reading Jensen's popular novel *Gradiva*, it is easy now in retrospect to detect the rich lode of ideas and imagery they provided for Freud. But, in the same way, if we look analytically at more mundane objects in the house, such as these sentimental images of Gastein, we find that they too can yield a seam of disturbing fantasies.

On the dining room wall by the veranda door hangs a print of **Fujiyama**
Mount Fuji. Dated 1929, it is by Kiyoshi Yoshida (1876-1956) and
was a gift to Freud in 1932 from the Japanese psychologist Heisaku
Kosawa, who was studying psychoanalysis in Europe.

Kosawa published a paper that year on the 'Ajase complex'
which he intended as a Japanese counterpart of the Oedipus complex. It refers to the tale of Prince Ajase who attempts to kill his
mother but falls sick with guilt and is saved only by her nursing.

Kosawa later founded a clinic in Tokyo. He was one of a
number of Japanese who imported Freud's ideas into Japan during
the 1930s, translated his work and in 1949 formed the Japanese
Society for Psychoanalytical Studies.

Two days after receiving Kosawa's gift, Freud wrote to him
on 20 February 1932 to thank him for 'the beautiful picture which
presents to my eyes what I have read so much about and a sight
which I myself have not been granted'. While the Bad Gastein
pictures on the same wall evoked a familiar past, this image
remained in the realm of the imagination and a reminder of
Freud's unfulfilled longing to travel the world.

Freud portraits: Schmutzer and Dali

Two portraits of Freud from two decades face us on the upper landing. The drawing above the table was a formal portrait done to celebrate his seventieth birthday in 1926. Freud afterwards wrote a letter of thanks to the artist, Ferdinand Schmutzer: 'My friends and relatives react either by admiring it at first sight or they find it initially too severe, only later gradually to admit that it becomes more and more like me. It gives me unusual joy and I feel obliged to thank you for the trouble you have taken to reproduce my ugly face...'

There is no record of Freud's reaction to the second portrait, hanging between two doors, or any certainty he ever saw it. The picture never belonged to him: it was donated to the museum in memory of its owner, Mrs Helene Eliat van de Velde, and it is the work of Salvador Dali who visited Freud on 22 July 1938 in the company of Stefan Zweig. In his memoirs Dali spoke of the inspiration for his picture while eating a meal of snails in France: 'All of a sudden I saw a photograph of Professor Freud on the front page of a newspaper which someone beside me was reading ... I uttered a loud cry. I had just that instant discovered the morphological secret of Freud! Freud's cranium is a snail! His brain is in the form of a spiral – to be extracted with a needle! This discovery strongly influenced the portrait drawing which I later made from life, a year before his death.'

Dali penned this finished portrait on blotting paper but it appears to have emerged from a series of preliminary pen sketches now in private collections. Where Dali had seen Freud's head as a snail, Stefan Zweig saw a skull in the sketches and was anxious that Freud should not see this foreboding of his imminent death.

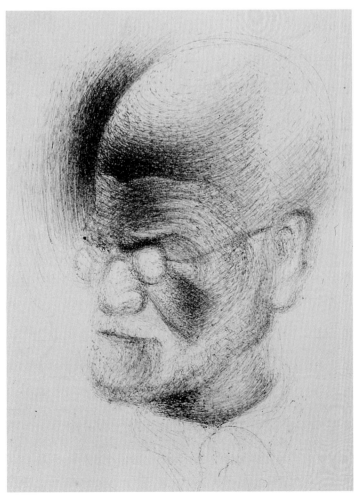

Anna Freud room

WHEN THE FAMILY emigrated to London it was Anna above all who had to deal with the Nazi bureaucracy and organize the practicalities. She had by this time become her father's chief helper and nurse. In the last six months of his life this meant rising several times in the night to apply Orthoform to his jaw as well as helping him each time he removed his prothesis for cleaning or to be examined. In spite of these tasks, she quickly settled down to work in her new home. She began seeing up to ten patients, working not only for herself but for the whole family as it tried to re-establish itself in London. She herself had described this type of personality under the concept of 'altruistic surrender' in her book, *The Ego and the Mechanisms of Defence* (1936); other people become the vicarious figures upon whom the subject has displaced his or her instinctual wishes.

Sigmund and Martha were near the end of their lives and Freud had even been prepared to remain in Austria despite the Nazis. It was partly in order to give Anna a new beginning that they had uprooted themselves. Soon after their arrival, she wrote to the American psychoanalyst Clinton McCord: 'England is indeed a civilised country and I am naturally grateful that we are here. There is no pressure of any kind and there is a great deal of space and freedom ahead.' Like many refugees, she threw herself heart and soul into her new life and by March 1939 she was writing to Ernst Simmel: 'Sometimes I seem to myself as though I were at least a thousand years old and already had several lifetimes behind me.'

When her father finally decided to end his intolerable suffering, he put his life in Anna's hands, for he told the doctor, Max Schur, to discuss the decision with her. After his death, her identification with him and his thought preserved his image in her mind and sustained her in her grief. 'He suffered greatly in the end, otherwise he was unchanged. I do not think he worried in the least how we would carry on without him. I think he thought we should have learned enough by now to manage alone,' she wrote to the American analyst, Brill on 27 December 1939. She also began to collect together all of her father's correspondence from his friends around the world, and to file his papers and manuscripts.

Her work left her little time to mourn: she had her adult practice and she was lecturing on child psychology in English. Child analysis had remained relatively uncharted territory in the 1920s and 1930s. Despite Freud's early study of 'Little Hans', the psychoanalytic understanding of children came largely from the analysis of adult patients. This gave only a partial view of children's development and offered no clues as to the analytic methods required to help them. Two of Anna's mentors in child psychology, Siegfried Bernfeld and August Aichhorn, had both had practical experience of dealing with children. Anna herself had started her career as a schoolteacher and began analytic work with children in 1923. Her first book in 1927 was a series of lectures for teachers and parents, entitled *Introduction to the Technique of Child Analysis*.

Meanwhile the Austrian, Melanie Klein, already in England, was evolving her own theory of early development and another technique of child analysis. She differed from Anna Freud as to the timing of the development of object relations and internalized structures. Also, she put the Oedipal stage much earlier, and considered the death drive to be of fundamental importance in infancy. After Anna's arrival in London, the conflict between their respective approaches threatened to split the British Psycho-Analytical Society. This was resolved through a series of wartime 'Controversial Discussions' that ended with the formation of parallel training courses for the two groups which continue to this day.

After the outbreak of war, Anna set up the War Nurseries in Hampstead and Essex, providing foster care for over eighty children from families dislocated by war. The children who came to the nurseries were often confused and traumatized. She soon discovered that air raids, bombs and the destruction of their former

Bomb-shelter bunks at the Hampstead War Nursery

homes and neighbourhoods were not the decisive causes of their suffering; it was the separation from their families which had the greatest traumatic effect. She aimed to help the children form attachments by providing continuity of relationships with the helpers and by encouraging mothers to visit as often as possible. Such attitudes were little heard of at the time, and the nurseries became, in effect, an imaginative experiment in meeting the developmental and emotional needs of infants and young children in long-term residential care.

'I have been especially fortunate all my life,' she wrote: 'From the very beginning, I was able to move back and forth

between practice and theory.' The stories of her nursery children's experiences were touchingly and often amusingly told in *Young Children in War-Time* and *Infants without Families* which she wrote together with Dorothy Burlingham. Out of the horror of war came an understanding of children and childcare which is still influential today.

The War Nursery in Essex

There was a further opportunity after the war to observe even more extreme parental deprivation. A group of orphans from the Theresienstadt concentration camp came into the care of Anna Freud's colleagues at the Bulldogs Bank home in Sussex and Anna Freud wrote about the children's ability to find substitute affections among their peers, in *An Experiment in Group Upbringing*.

In 1947 she and Kate Friedlaender established the Hampstead Child Therapy Courses, and a children's clinic was added five years later. Now that she was training English and American child therapists, her influence in the field grew rapidly. Her technique

involved the use of developmental lines charting theoretical normal growth 'from dependency to emotional self-reliance' or 'from
play to work' and so on. 'Diagnostic profiles' enabled the analyst
to separate and identify the specific factors that deviated from, or
conformed to, normal development. These developmental lines
seemed very simple. In fact, they synthesized different aspects of
Freudian metapsychology into an accessible behavioural description. However, she always took into account the unconscious factors that determined the meaning and pattern of any particular
developmental phase. Thus, in the development 'from suckling to
rational eating', the attitude to food may in one instance be moti-
vated by the relation to the mother, and in another by sexual theories and phantasies. Different treatment options would be suggested in each case.

In one respect, Anna Freud differed markedly from her
father. Her concept of 'normality' as a standard by which to meas-
ure deviations in development does not match Freud's aim of
closing the 'supposed gap' between normality and pathology. In
many ways, her practical cast of mind lent itself to this outlook.
As a child she disliked fairy stories because they were not 'true'.
She required a stable point of reference from which to view the
world – a necessity perhaps when faced with the daily tasks of
training and supervising at the Hampstead Clinic.

Practical tasks constantly clamoured for her attention. A
nursery school was added to the clinic at Maresfield Gardens. A
dismal basement was transformed by Anna's brother Ernst into a
bright and welcoming environment. After the first few years the
nursery began to take on deprived children from the local area,
and the close association with the clinic provided invaluable support. Soon there was a Well Baby Clinic, a Nursery School for
Blind Children and a Mother and Toddler Group. The nursery
workers were encouraged to make a daily record of anything that
struck their attention, and became adept at the art of close observation. 'Usually the children are expected to adjust to the nursery,'
a clinic worker said, 'in our nursery the teachers adjust to the
child.' Many of these observations were incorporated into Anna
Freud's *Normality and Pathology in Childhood*.

From the 1950s until the end of her life, Anna Freud travelled
regularly to the United States to lecture, teach and visit friends.
During the 1970s she was concerned with the problems of working
with emotionally deprived and socially disadvantaged children,

Anna Freud and Dorothy Burlingham with their American colleagues, Albert Solnit and Joseph Goldstein

and she studied deviations and delays in development. At Yale Law School she taught seminars on crime and the family and collaborated with Joseph Goldstein and Albert Solnit in writing a study of children and the law, *Beyond the Best Interests of the Child* (1973).

She also received many honorary doctorates, the first of which was awarded in 1950 by Clark University where her father had lectured in 1909, the last by Harvard in 1980. In 1967 she was made a CBE. Like her father, she regarded awards less as personal recognition and more as honours for psychoanalysis. And although she accepted the praise with good grace and characteristic humour, she commented that speeches about her achievements made her feel as if she were already dead.

Of her father's work, Anna Freud said: 'We felt that we were the first who had been given a key to the understanding of human behaviour and its aberrations as being determined not by overt factors but by the pressure of instinctual forces emanating from the unconscious mind...' Her life continued his intellectual adventure. Above all, she sought useful social applications of psychoanalysis in treating, and learning from, children. She left her legacy in her writings, in the clinic she formed and directed, and in the memories of those who knew her.

Dorothy Burlingham

When Anna Freud opened a nursery school in Vienna in 1937, one of her co-workers was the American Dorothy Burlingham. Both women devoted their lives to the study of children and their friendship lasted over fifty years. Although Dorothy lived at 20 Maresfield Gardens for many years a photograph of her hanging behind the loom is one of the very few visible signs of that vital relationship. One reason for this is that Dorothy was by nature shy and retiring. She had come to Vienna in the 1920s because her marriage had broken up and both she and her children needed treatment. Her family moved into the flat above the Freuds at Berggasse 19 and the two households lived in what Freud termed 'symbiosis'. Her children attended the small Hietzing School run on psychoanalytical lines and she began a psychoanalytical practice.

Her first patient was a blind girl and when she came to London with the Freuds she was to continue working with, and writing about, blind children. At the War Nurseries and the

Hampstead Clinic, Anna and Dorothy worked together. Dorothy moved into Maresfield Gardens and she and Anna together bought a summer cottage in the East Anglian village of Walberswick, which was to replace the loss of their country cottage near Vienna. Despite occasional speculations that their relationship was actively sexual, all the evidence points to a platonic partnership, albeit one that was closer, more harmonious and longer-lasting than most marriages. Dorothy was the younger sister of twins and as an adult she studied the behaviour of twin children: the relationship with Anna was like that of twin sisters.

The wooden loom that stands in the Anna Freud room continued in use. When Anna died she bequeathed it to her friend Manna Friedman, a previous director of the Anna Freud Nursery school, who wove rugs. These were sold to benefit the Anna Freud Clinic, a tradition started by Anna herself in 1981 when she first sold knitting and weaving produced by herself and friends in aid of the clinic. Her weaving was therefore both useful and therapeutic, for it calmed her and helped her to concentrate, in much the same way

Weaving

as her father needed cigars to help him work. She even composed lectures at the loom.

The activity of weaving has given language some of its profoundest metaphors. Past and present are 'woven together' or we speak of a 'weave' of personal and social relations. The literary text (like 'textile') comes from weaving. One of Freud's wilder speculations attributes the invention of weaving to women and to the unconscious effect of 'penis envy'. Weaving imitates the pubic hair concealing the genitals, hence it is associated with shame and with a 'substitute penis'. Recognizing how bizarre this sounds, Freud added: 'If you reject this idea as fantastic and regard my belief in the influence of lack of penis on the configuration of femininity as an *idée fixe*, I am of course defenceless.' [SE XXII.132]

Wolf and the dogs

A photo of the Alsatian called Wolf, together with a poem, was presented to Freud on his seventieth birthday in 1926. It now hangs in the room dedicated to Anna Freud since Wolf was her dog and the poem was written by her, in the dog's name.

> *Because so many other relatives have come*
> *Someone who's been banished from the home*
> *Is dumbly paying his respects today*
> *In contrast to his usual noisy way.*
> *His love for everything that's friendly and edible*
> *Is not even with swallowed thermometers measurable,*
> *So out of the nourishing things at the feast retain*
> *His share of the remains.*
> *He greets you, despite the transience of every delicacy,*
> *With unchanging doggy fidelity.*

Wolf had been acquired in 1925 and was the first of the Freud dogs: his poem was also to be the first of a series of dog poems presented to Freud on subsequent birthdays.

In 1928 Freud was given his own dog, the chow bitch Lun Yug, for late in life he had become a dog lover. When this dog died in an accident the following year he was saddened and it needed months of persuasion before he was ready for a replacement, another chow bitch called Jofi who arrived early in 1930. He became extremely attached to her and she was his constant companion for the next six years. During psychoanalytical hours she

**Opposite page:
Freud with his chow Jofi
during the 1930s**

lay at his feet and, according to family folklore, Freud would know exactly when the hour was over since she would get up at precisely the right time. It was also said that he used her to 'vet' potential patients: if she was suspicious of them or turned away from them, they were considered unsuitable candidates for treatment.

When Jofi died early in 1937 Freud mourned her almost like a child. 'But of course one cannot easily get over seven years' of intimacy,' he wrote to Arnold Zweig on 10 February. This time, however, he quickly acquired a replacement chow, Lun, who was to come to England with him. In Freud's very last weeks, the dog was repelled by the smell from his cancerous mouth. This rejection grieved Freud, perhaps not so much as a portent of death, but because it signified the loss of one of his closest bonds of affection.

Apart from the yearly poems, the dogs left another literary trace. Princess Marie Bonaparte who had first alerted Freud to the merits of chows, had written a short book about the illness of her chow, Topsy. Ironically this dog also had cancer and was treated by a radiologist who was later to be consulted on Freud's case. Sigmund and Anna Freud together translated this book into German. Work on it helped to pass the long days in Nazi Vienna, waiting for their emigration papers to arrive. The translation appeared in May 1939, a week before the English translation of *Moses and Monotheism*.

On the far wall of the Anna Freud room hangs an embroidered picture of a chow. After her father's death Anna continued to keep chows for the rest of her life and each was given the name Jofi. Her friend Alice Colonna was to inherit one of these Jofis and, during Anna Freud's final illness, she made this picture as a gift and consolation for its ailing mistress.

Video room

Freud recording a talk for the BBC on 7 December 1938

THE PRESENT VIDEO ROOM was previously a bedroom – a place of darkness and dreams. Now films are shown there, notably the *Home Movies*, documentary footage of Freud and his family in the 1930s. Their images are moving in both senses of the word. The Freud we see is certainly himself, yet, as in dreams, there is a difference between the familiar figure and the image. What has become the stereotypical Freud is a stern, almost accusing, face that stares out at us from thousands of book jackets. The Freud who moves through the film often smiles. He seems far gentler and more sympathetic than that punitive intellectual icon.

One reason for this is that he is shown in his home surroundings, among family and friends and dogs. When posing for formal portraits Freud always put on a stern face. But here the footage was informally shot, sometimes even without his knowledge, and by friends – Ruth and Mark Brunswick and Princess Marie Bonaparte. The film itself was put together out of fragments, in part to give Anna Freud a window on her own past when the Hampstead Clinic (now the Anna Freud Centre) celebrated its twentieth anniversary. Later she added her own commentary, and her words, those of an old woman looking back at her past life, add historical depth and resonance.

After the end of the film, Freud himself is heard, the only known recording of his voice, made by the BBC on 7 December 1938. Because of the unwieldy prosthesis the tone is muffled but the words are uttered clearly with a slight accent. The delivery is slow, rhythmic and forceful. In a nutshell he provides us with his own summary of his life's work:

'I started my professional activity as a neurologist, trying to bring relief to my neurotic patients. Under the influence of an older friend and by my own efforts I discovered some new and important facts about the Unconscious in psychic life, the role of instinctual urges and so on. Out of these findings grew a new science, Psycho-Analysis, a part of Psychology and a new method of treatment of the neuroses.

I had to pay heavily for this bit of good luck. People did not believe in my facts and thought my theories unsavoury. Resistance was strong and unrelenting. In the end I succeeded in acquiring pupils and building up an International Psycho-Analytic Association. But the struggle is not yet over.'

Freud's mother

In the opening scenes of the *Home Movies* we see Freud's mother, who was born in 1835 and died in 1930. She was only twenty-one when he was born; he was the first and best loved of all her children. 'A man who has been his mother's undisputed favourite goes into life with a confidence of success which often brings actual success along with it,' Freud wrote. Later scenes in the film show Freud with three grandsons, Stephen, Lucian and Clement. This historical span puts his life into a wider perspective: we see him not just as father and husband, but as son and grandfather.

His mother's death preceded his own by only nine years and until that time one of his greatest fears was that he might die

Freud's mother Amalia
as a younger woman.
Anna Freud said: 'My
grandmother was very
concerned with looking
nice and not too old.'

before her. He could not bear the thought that she might have to be told of his death. And so when she did die, he reacted with relief: now that she was gone he was at last free to die himself.

Going back to his infancy – in one of the very few incidents he told about his mother – we find that she was the one who taught him the most important fact of life. The story comes in *The Interpretation of Dreams*; it happened when he was six and his mother was giving him his first lessons. She told him that we are all made of earth and must therefore return to the earth. The little boy didn't like this and expressed his doubts, whereupon she rubbed her palms together and showed him black scales of dead skin produced by the friction. Freud wrote of his astonishment at this demonstration. Convinced she was right, he realized then that he owed nature a death.

Cigars

1920, Freud with cigar
in Holland, the smoker's
paradise

Virtually every portrait of Freud depicts him holding a cigar. He
had been a lifelong heavy smoker and when he was later forced to
stop (only temporarily, for he was too much of an addict to give it
up for long), he complained that he was unable to work and that
his creativity was bound up with his smoking He 'owed to cigars
the greater part of his self-discipline and steadfastness at work', he
wrote to Stefan Zweig on 7 February 1931.

But there was a heavy price to pay. That smoking caused his
mouth cancer could hardly be disputed, yet Freud never renounced
or denounced (or analyzed) his addiction. The first surgical
attempt to contain the disease was an unsuccessful and almost
fatal operation early in 1923. The treatment was subsequently
taken over by a very competent surgeon, Hans Pichler. There is no

doubt that Pichler's prompt excision of all threatening growths extended Freud's life far beyond the five years or so predicted. Over the next fifteen years of constant treatment, which included thirty operations and innumerable consultations, Pichler was able to contain the disease, but at a high cost to the patient who stoically endured repeated painful surgery and the perpetual discomfort of successive ill-fitting prostheses.

It was not the cancer, but heart trouble, which caused Freud to cut down smoking in his later years. But he could never give up the habit entirely, and it remained one of the great pleasures of his life.

'My father didn't like to be photographed and usually made a face when he noticed it.' Anna Freud's comment about a scene in the *Home Movies* gives a clue to the development of a certain image of Freud as stern, unyielding and tyrannical. Most of the well-known portraits were commissioned by him from his son-in-law Max Halberstadt during the 1920s, partly as a favour to help his dead daughter's widower through a difficult period. These images are

Freud's smile

Freud in Berlin, 1929, with Anna, his sister Mitzi and her grand-daughter Angela indeed forbidding but they are in stark contrast to the smiling Freud of the film.

Freud, like Einstein, has become a twentieth-century myth and a myth attaches itself to an iconic image. The amiable, dog-loving old man of the *Home Movies* presents another angle on his personality, although without necessarily destroying that fixed image. Nevertheless, it is important to 'confuse the picture' a little and show as many sides of Freud as possible, not only of his work but of his biography. Disciples and detractors alike return again and again to the question of his personality – whether he was a fearless pioneer or a fraudulent deluder who managed to impose his theses on both his patients and the world. Too often the argument around psychoanalysis degenerates into a simplistic antithesis, a play of idealized or demonic projections.

For the time being Freud's shadow still falls heavily across our times. But advances in science and developments in psycho-therapy will inevitably modify Freudian psychology. As that system shifts in its historical and cultural contexts, so too will his smile and frown alter in their iconographic meanings.

Freud in 1905 with Martha and Minna, his mother in the background

Exhibition room

THE HOUSE OF A GREAT MAN attracts us because we seek contact with the reality of his ideas. But the reality of Freud's ideas takes us into the unreality of our own perceptions, thoughts and dreams. The museum can only exhibit fragments or aspects of Freud's ideas without claiming or hoping to give an overview. Perhaps psychoanalysis by its nature defies such a perspective.

Freud himself was only too aware of the limits to the representability of ideas. One of his own dreams, from *The Interpretation of Dreams* illustrates the nature of the difficulty: 'Old Brücke must have set me some task; strangely enough, it related to a dissection of the lower part of my body, my pelvis and legs, which I saw before me as though in the dissecting-room, but without noticing their absence in myself and also without a trace of any gruesome feeling.' [SE V:452]

This self-dissection was Freud's self-analysis: it is a graphic image of the contradiction involved in being objective about subjective experience. That was one obstacle he had to overcome. Another was that to exhibit his own dreams was an act of self-exposure at odds with his usual reticence. But the essence of psychoanalysis is exposure of the hidden, despite personal or social resistances.

Another of his own dreams depicted an open-air toilet. 'The seat (except, of course, for the hole) was an exact copy of a piece of furniture which had been given to me as a present by a grateful woman patient. It thus reminded me of how much my patients honoured me. Indeed, even the museum of human excrement could be given an interpretation to rejoice my heart.' [SE V:469]

What sort of real exhibit or museum could do justice to such dislocations of reality – bowels revealed as an object of study or the couch transformed into a toilet?

In the 1920s the German film director, Georg-Wilhelm Pabst, was working on a film based on psychoanalysis. Freud's colleagues, Karl Abraham and Hanns Sachs, cooperated on the scenario but Freud was adamant in his refusal to have anything to do with the film. 'In my judgement,' he wrote to Ernst Simmel on

26 October 1925, 'analysis does not lend itself to any kind of cinematic representation.' Later he was to offer a vertiginous example of the limits of representability: this is the image of memory which he depicts in *Civilization and Its Discontents*. He takes Rome as his analogy and proceeds to slice through it in space and time simultaneously. He calls the attempt a phantasy and adds

> If we want to represent historical sequence in spatial terms we
> can only do it by juxtaposition in space: the same space can-
> not have two different contents. Our attempt seems to be an
> idle game. It has only one justification. It shows us how
> far we are from mastering the characteristics of mental life by
> representing them in pictorial terms.

In the end he concludes: 'The fact remains that only in the mind is such a preservation of all the earlier stages alongside the final form possible, and that we are not in a position to represent this phenomenon in pictorial terms.' [SE XXI.70-71]

Finally, in the context of this museum and the ideas it represents (but cannot exhibit), here is another of Freud's architectural metaphors. Discussing their respective angles on personality, Freud wrote to Ludwig Binswanger on 8 October 1936; 'I have always lived on the ground floor and in the basement of the building – you maintain that on changing one's viewpoint one can also see an upper floor housing such distinguished guests as religion, art and others.' At Maresfield Gardens Freud's study is literally on the ground floor. This house-museum is a place where some ideas and metaphors are real.

Exhibitions

Freud's exile, Viennese culture, Freud in England, the life and work of Anna Freud, archaeology, and, of course, Freud's own work: these have all been the themes of some of the temporary exhibitions held in the museum. Numerous travelling exhibitions and museums both in the U.K. and abroad have also been dedicated to Freud and his antiquities. These collaborative exhibitions have resulted in catalogues such as *Freud and Art*, *Freud's Sculpture*, *"Meine… alten und dreckigen Götter": aus Freuds Sammlung* and *La passion à l'œuvre: Rodin et Freud collectionneurs*. The international significance of Freud's work is reflected in the list of venues – USA, Japan, Brazil, Belgium, the Netherlands, Austria, Mexico, Italy, Portugal, France, Germany and Australia.

Freud and psychoanalysis are cultural phenomena that have had a vital influence on the arts. Consequently exhibition themes have not been limited to antiquities, Freud's theory and biography. The museum has also developed a close relationship with contemporary art. The Museum celebrated its tenth anniversary in 1996 by producing a folio of ten prints by ten eminent living artists – Peter Blake, Patrick Caulfield, Prunella Clough, Susan Hiller, Matthew Hilton, Joseph Kosuth, Claes Oldenburg, Cornelia Parker, Alison Watt and Paul Wunderlich – each of whom created a new work inspired by the Freud Museum. Since that year the museum has put on over forty individual or group art exhibitions, occasionally in collaboration with the nearby Camden Arts Centre. The artists include Susan Hiller, Sarah Lucas, Sophie Calle, Ralph Freeman, Stuart Brisley, Valie Export, Vera Frenkel, Ellen Gallagher, Tim Noble and Sue Webster, Oliver Clegg and Matt Collishaw. Further details of all these exhibitions can be found on the museum website at: www.freud.org.uk/exhibitions/archive.

Susan Hiller's SOPHIA/*wisdom*. Detail from the exhibition *At the Freud Museum* (1992)

This conjunction of psychoanalysis and art at the museum has also resulted in a number of books and exhibition catalogues, such as Paul Coldwell's *Freud's Coat*, Susan Hiller's *After the Freud Museum*, Sophie Calle's *Appointment with Sigmund Freud*, Jane McAdam *Freud's Relative Relations*, Vivienne Koorland's *Reisemalheurs* and William Cobbing's *Gradiva Project*. Over the years the exhibitions of contemporary art at the Freud Museum have attracted great interest in the art world, and they have themselves become a topic of academic study.

The study

AN ATMOSPHERE IS INSTANTLY sensed but not so easily explained. Because the museum is the scene of Freud's absent presence, every visitor can project his or her own emotions onto the study or free associate on the images and objects on display. This is not just a subjective process: the design of the museum encourages one's sense of gaining privileged access to a secret place. The shop is at the back of the house to prevent commerce interfering with the experience. Similarly, objects in the study are unlabelled to maintain the effect of visiting a private house. Information gives way to evocation, which is a different kind of knowledge.

Nevertheless, the privileged access is not complete. Guide ropes are barriers between the visitor and the study and this taboo on touching plays a part in generating the atmosphere of the museum. That atmosphere is founded on multiple impressions: the muted light in the study, the colour and smell of carpets, the mustiness of old books, the indefinable interplay of expectation and experience, memory and imagination. Some visitors experience the study as a womb, as if Freud encapsulated himself in a little bubble that protected him from everyday cares and worries; for others it is like a tomb. The fact that the curtains have to be kept closed (for conservation and security reasons) contributes to these impressions. Yet Freud loved the brightness of the house and would in fact have worked with the garden windows open as much as possible. The crowded objects, especially on the desk, may seem oppressive. But a switch of angle may transmute depressive or oppressive aspects of the atmosphere into liberation from mourning and anxiety. In one of his own dream-analyses Freud connected his wish for immortality through his work with a visit to an Etruscan grave near Orvieto. The clustered antiquities and the dark ranks of library books surrounding the study are windows opening into the bright light of world culture.

Culture and science involve classification. There are nearly as many possibilities for classification as there are objects in the study. Apart from furniture, rugs, books and pictures, the antiquities themselves offer numerous possibilities. We might classify them according to their origins in Egypt, Greece, Rome or the Far East and our associations to these places will colour our interpretation of what the classification means. We might classify according to function – funerary objects, everyday objects and so on, or according to mythological themes associated with the objects.

Freud's print of the Orvieto graves. 'For I had already been in a grave once, but it was an excavated Etruscan grave near Orvieto...' [SE V.454]

Over and above that there are more abstract characteristics which could be broadly characterised as 'exotic' or 'mundane', 'far off' and 'familiar'. Contemplation of the antiquities reminded Freud of distant places and cultures and offered him insights and inspiration.

Many house-museums preserve entire buildings apparently unchanged, as monuments to their famous inhabitants. The Freud Museum is a 'compromise formation', an attempt to solve conflicts between mental events and the outside world. The museum must combine the intimacy of a private house with the demands of a public exhibition space. This in itself preserves something of the sense of the house as it was lived in, since, during Freud's lifetime, many of his patients said that the atmosphere was more like that of a museum than a private house. And there is also the sense in which Freud cannot be reduced to a private individual. His work is not just public property; it has become part of our most ingrained habits of thought. As Auden's elegy for him states, 'He has become a climate of opinion.'

Are there elements in the study which correspond to Freud's conception of the ego, id and superego? Or would it be more appropriate to think of personality traits? Certainly an obsessional personality may leave his or her mark on the layout and structure of a room which conveys itself to the person who visits it. Similarly we may suddenly be aware of a profound sense of loss covered over by a multitude of objects, just as depressive sadness may be covered by a superficial gaiety. Other visitors may suddenly feel frightened and not know why. The mummy mask at the foot of the couch, the sense that the objects may be watching you, the sheer oppressive feel of so much history may all contribute to an atmosphere which echoes a paranoid personality. Freud's insistence on digging ever deeper into the mire of human motives and his quest to find things out certainly bears out his view that the structure of science is closely connected to the structure of paranoia. Both the scientist and the paranoiac cannot help themselves asking 'why?'

If the atmosphere of Freud's study contains the spirit of Freud, it is not in a mystical way but as a concrete embodiment of who he was. In visiting the museum we communicate with Freud as one unconscious relating to another. But we have a choice in our attitude. Either we can let this happen without conscious awareness, or we can carry forward the spirit of his work: 'Psychoanalysis is an instrument to enable the ego to achieve a progressive conquest of the id.' [SE XIX.56]

The couch is one of the most famous pieces of furniture in the **The couch**
world. It has come to represent the practice of psychoanalysis. But
it also represents the uncertain space that psychoanalysis occupies.
Negatively defined, that space is neither medicine nor psychiatry,
neither religious confession nor artistic creation. Yet it involves
aspects of all of these.

When Freud began his medical practice in Vienna in 1886, he
initially used the conventional treatments of the time – electrotherapy, massage and therapeutic baths – all of them physical
methods. Disappointment with those current therapies led him to
seek more effective cures. Charcot had already alerted him to hypnosis and the effect of ideas on nervous disorders and in 1889 he
visited Liébeault and Bernheim in Nancy to study their hypnotic
treatments. For several years after that he used hypnosis on many
of his patients. But the amazing cures it sometimes brought about

were generally followed by relapses.

It was in 1891 that a grateful patient, Mrs Benvenisti, apparently gave Freud the couch as a gift. He was still only a medical doctor who happened to specialize in nervous disorders. At the time his mentor was Josef Breuer and they discussed the hysteric cases Freud was dealing with and which were to be published in *Studies in Hysteria*. It was the earliest of those cases, Breuer's 'Anna O', who invented 'the talking cure': she had decided to dictate her own method of treatment to the doctor by relating the experiences that led to her sickness. Following her example, Freud found that by letting his own patients remember and speak of the trauma that had caused their condition he could effect a temporary alleviation of their trouble. This was to be termed the 'cathartic method'.

Because blocked memories could not be forced, Freud later came to adopt a technique of getting round repression by 'free association' – letting the patient say whatever came to mind and then interpreting the unconscious messages and memories the words conveyed. Patients needed to be completely relaxed and so it became customary for them to lie on the couch as an aid to free association.

Two different accounts exist of why the therapist's chair came to be positioned behind the patient. One was that a patient had once tried to make advances to the doctor: the other is simply, as Freud told Hanns Sachs, 'I cannot let myself be stared at for eight hours daily.' The two accounts are not contradictory, since both refer in different ways to the same necessity of keeping an emotional distance between therapist and patient.

As a piece of domestic furniture, the couch continues to remind us of the relation between home and surgery, between the patient's life and the illness. Before Freud these areas had been kept separate. The patient was treated physically, as an object of study for the doctor. By listening to his patients, Freud linked all their subjective experiences to the objective moment of therapy. The fact that dreams and everyday life were the material of this new psychology made it accessible to everyone. Artists and writers, whether surrealist, modernist or realist, were fascinated by it and their work helped to publicize and popularize the psycho-analytic movement. The couch has become a symbol for psychoanalysis itself as the place where the unconscious reveals itself in speech.

Two images of the French doctor Jean-Martin Charcot (1825-1893) watch over Freud's study. The most striking hangs above the couch: a lithograph of André Brouillet's painting, *Une Leçon Clinique à la Salpêtrière*. It shows Charcot presenting to a class his most famous hysterical patient, Blanche Wittman. When exhibited at the Paris Salon in 1887 the enormous painting attracted half a million visitors and copies of it were extremely popular.

Charcot

In the painting Charcot is using his hypnotic technique in order to demonstrate the features of hysterical attacks as he painstakingly identified and described them. Wittman is depicted in a scanty low-cut chemise with her corset loosened, seductively swooning into the arms of Babinski, one of Charcot's most famous disciples. Charcot, at her side, addresses the rapt, all-male audience, a group of doctors known collectively as the Salpêtrière school.

Brouillet has captured, perhaps inadvertently, the subtle interplay of power and sexuality in the patient-doctor relationship which was to have such a profound influence on the development of psychoanalysis. The doctors lean forward, waiting expectantly for something to happen. All eyes are on the patient to confirm Charcot's diagnosis and clinical description. For a brief moment the reputation of the doctor rests in her hands. What if she refuses to be hypnotized? But the forces of suggestion and the highly-charged atmosphere of the hospital are mobilized for the benefit of the doctor's authority, to allow the self-fulfilling prophecy to take place.

When Freud visited Paris in 1885-86 as a young doctor on a travelling scholarship, Charcot, the 'Napoleon of the neuroses', was at the height of his fame. Freud had come to study neuro-pathology under Charcot's direction. Here he learned the effect of hypnosis in producing and removing hysterical symptoms, which indicated to him that the disorder had a psychogenic rather than a physical origin.

Freud's daughter Mathilde once asked what was wrong with the woman in Brouillet's picture. He replied that she was too tightly laced. This phrase summarizes Freud's own lesson at the Salpêtrière. It was there that Charcot first gave him an inkling of the effects of sexual repression. In the *History of the Psychoanalytic Movement* Freud reports his amazement that Charcot knew this, for he heard him say 'c'est toujours la chose génitale' ('it's always to do

with the genitals') without ever wanting to make his discovery public.

The other image on the far wall is a signed photograph of Charcot. Freud translated some of Charcot's works on hysteria into German and this picture was a token of the master's gratitude. Freud's early theory of hysteria differed from Charcot's in its insistence on an origin in psycho-sexual trauma, yet he continued to respect him, particularly for his insistence on painstaking empirical observation. In 1889 Freud named his first son Jean-Martin in Charcot's honour.

The chair

Visitors to the study are intrigued by the armchair behind the desk. Its sculptural curves and rounded headrest are reminiscent of a Henry Moore figure. This curiously-shaped chair was made for Freud in 1930 by the architect Felix Augenfeld, as a gift from Freud's daughter Mathilde. Augenfeld wrote: 'She explained to me that S.F. had the habit of reading in a very peculiar and uncomfortable body position. He was leaning in this chair, in some sort of diagonal position, one of his legs slung over the arm of the chair, the book held high and his head unsupported. The rather bizarre form of the chair I designed is to be explained as an attempt to maintain this habitual posture and to make it more comfortable.'

The armrests doubled as legrests and the high back served Freud the reader, not the writer.

The desk

In Vienna Freud's study and consulting room were separate: in London they are the same room, and one which opens out into the garden he loved. Rows of antiquities crowd his desk, an audience that hardly seems to leave space for the writing. Useful bric-à-brac, jade bowls and ashtrays, cigar box, inkstand and penholder, occupy the rest of the free surface, so that there is only just room for the large A3 sheets of unlined paper on which Freud wrote. It is as if the museum atmosphere of his Vienna home were concentrated here on the desk, and this plenitude of artefacts and cultural references crowding him in were a necessary source of inspiration.

The layout of rooms may illustrate their inhabitant's position in the world of ideas. The couch and bookshelves opposite the desk, for example, fix Freud's position between theory and therapy. He described psychoanalysis 'as a procedure for the treatment of nervous diseases, as a method of research and as an auxiliary instrument for scientific work in the most various departments of intellectual life'.[SE XIX.214] And he expressed his hope 'that the therapy will not destroy the science'. From this remark it could even be deduced that Freud's allegiance to theory might be stronger than his commitment to therapy.

At the age of eighteen Freud had written to his friend Eduard Silberstein: 'I am one of those human beings who can be found most of the day between two pieces of furniture, one formed vertically, the armchair, and one extending horizontally, the table, and from these, as social historians are agreed, sprang all civilization...' Seven year later, during his engagement, he sent Martha a diagram of his room, with the work area labelled the 'animal side' and the sleeping area the 'vegetative side'. In the same letter he compared his own brain to a room or warehouse full of medical cases, theories and diagnoses. This is an early illustration of Freud's 'topological imagination', that is, his way of linking abstract ideas to spatial relations.

Freud's scientific apprenticeship is represented by three portraits in the study. They are of Hermann Helmholtz, Ernst Wilhelm von Brücke and Ernst von Fleischl-Marxow, the men he most respected during his years as a student and a research physiologist (1873-86).

Portraits in the study

Freud never met **Hermann von Helmholtz** (1821-1894), one of the most important scientists of the nineteenth century *(right)*. He was one of a scientific group who revolutionized physiology. They stated that all forces within the organism should be explained by chemical or physical causes inherent in matter and that these could be reduced to the force of attraction and repulsion. They opposed the pseudo-mystical 'vital forces' terminology so popular at the time. Freud accepted their determinism and aimed at first to develop his own theories on that basis.

Ernst Wilhelm von Brücke (1819-1892), Professor of Physiology at Vienna University, Freud's teacher and Director of the Physiological Institute where

Freud worked as a demonstrator between 1876 and 1882, Brücke *(left)* belonged to 'Helmholtz's School of Medicine' and taught Freud the scientific grounding which was to serve him all his life. In 1927, in his postscript to *The Question of Lay Analysis*, Freud said that Brücke '...carried more weight with me than any one else in my whole life'. Perhaps this idealized portrait indicates that the scientific 'father' stood in for Freud's real, and weaker, father. After Brücke's death in 1892, Freud named his second son Ernst in his memory.

Ernst von Fleischl-Marxow (1847-1891), physicist and physiologist *(below)*, was a brilliant young assistant to Ernst Brücke at his Physiological Institute. Nine years older than Freud, von Fleischl-Marxow was a senior colleague when Freud became a demonstrator at the Physiological Institute (1876-1882). He later became a close friend and a personal and intellectual ideal for Freud. Von Fleischl-Marxow suffered intense pain from an amputated thumb following infection during a dissection. His treatment by morphine supposedly led to addiction, though it seems likely he had already been using the drug

before the injury. Freud sought to treat the addiction with cocaine, believing that to be a cure for morphinism. The high dosage of cocaine needed, however, led in turn to delirium and a pitiful end. Freud was deeply affected by his friend's suffering. '...I admire and love him with an intellectual passion...' he wrote to Martha on 28 October 1883. 'His destruction will move me as the destruction of a sacred and famous temple would have affected an ancient Greek.'

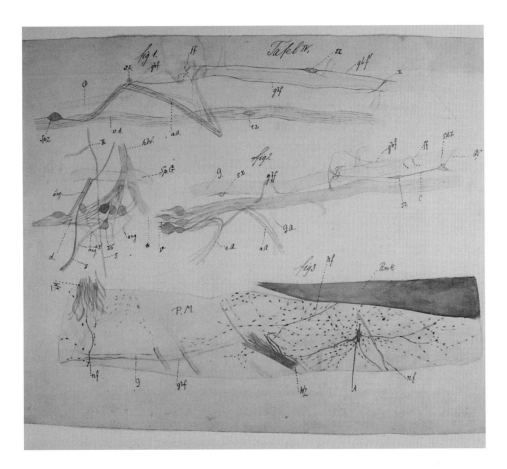

Freud's first scientific publication appeared in 1877, on the structure of nerve cells in Petromyzon, a primitive type of fish. In it Freud established the evolutionary continuity of nerve structure between primitive and higher animals. Though his field of research was to change radically in years to come, the scientific undercurrent remained consistent with this first work – the search for origins and the application of evolutionary principles.

Petromyzon and after

Freud studied medicine, but as a young graduate had no clear idea of his future career. His first preference was for physiological research in the laboratory of Ernst Brücke at Vienna University. Had his family been rich he might have continued here indefinitely. However, Brücke finally warned him that it would be many years before he could expect to make money in that field. And since, by that time, Freud had became engaged, he needed to establish himself financially in order to marry.

Thus he chose to go into private practice. As part of his training he resolved to study surgery and so spent a couple of years as resident doctor at the General Hospital in Vienna. He served first under Nothnagel in his Division of Internal Medicine. But Freud had always lacked enthusiasm for medicine as such. He had initially been interested in anatomical research and had hoped to make his name in this field. In 1879 he had published a paper on his discovery of a new method of staining specimens of nerve tissue to prepare them for microscopic examination. He turned himself into a specialist on brain anatomy and pathology and the structure of the *medulla oblongata*. But his antipathy towards the practical side of medicine is shown by the fact that he put off completing his medical studies until 1881. Given his interest in neuro-pathology, it was hardly surprising that he was not keen on everyday hospital work. After six months under Nothnagel he transferred to Meynert's psychiatric clinic where he spent a further five months from May to September 1883, acquiring his first experience of the psychiatric medicine of the time.

Notes taken by doctors (including Freud) on patients at their admission bear witness to current diagnostic practice, which concentrated on physical symptoms and family pathology. Categories of insanity overlapped conceptually with aspects of physical illnesses; apart from noting heredity or alcohol abuse, little attempt was made to assign causes. Freud's turning away from psychiatry was an expression of dissatisfaction with its practice and methodology at the time.

The lost portrait

Freud's eldest son Martin wrote a memoir of life with his father and in it he states that there was a portrait of Wilhelm Fliess in the study. But no such portrait has been found, nor does it appear in any of the old photographs. The story behind this 'lost' portrait could serve as a psychoanalytic parable.

During the 1890s, the years during which Freud was developing psychoanalysis in 'splendid isolation', he was in fact in constant contact with the Berlin ear, nose and throat specialist, Wilhelm Fliess. In correspondence with him, Freud tried out all his new ideas. Fliess was in fact the vital transferential Other, the figure who witnessed and assisted his self-analysis.

At the beginning of the twentieth century, after the publication of *The Interpretation of Dreams*, the friendship ended in bitterness and recriminations. When Fliess's widow put their correspondence up for sale in 1936 Freud wanted it destroyed. It was saved by

Wilhelm Fliess (1858–1928), Freud's friend and correspondent from 1887 to 1904

Princess Marie Bonaparte who bought it but refused to hand it over to Freud. It is understandable that Freud would have been sensitive to having the failure of a friendship and his own early theoretical errors publicized. But was it likely that he would have rubbed salt into his own wounds by having a portrait of Fliess in front of him all those years? Or can we assume that Martin, who never knew Fliess, was confusing him with another of Freud's bearded mentors with a similar name, Fleischl, whose portrait always occupied a place of honour in the study?

It was to Fliess that Freud first momentously confessed that he no longer believed his patients' memories of early seduction. From that switch in perspective, psychoanalysis emerged as the study of the repressions, distortions and fantasies – the lost pictures that make up our psychic history.

The Roman Forum

For the artist, Luigi Kasimir, who made the print of the Roman Forum that hangs in the study, it may have signified nostalgia for the lost order of the classical world. Here, in this house, the image acquires a new set of meanings. Hanging where it does, above the head of the psycho-analyst's chair, it inevitably recalls the archaeological metaphor for psychoanalysis.

In the mind as in the world, the past perpetually glimmers through the present moment. In *Civilization and its Discontents* Freud tried to depict the spatio-temporal complexity of 'mental reality' by imagining that all the many stages of Rome's development were simultaneously visible: 'This would mean that in Rome the palaces of the Caesars and the Septizonium of Septimus Severus would still be rising to their old height on the Palatine... Where the Coliseum now stands we could at the same time admire Nero's vanished Golden house...'

In Freud's house this picture of peaceful ruins signifies the confusing reality of the psyche, in which past and present, with all their traumas and desires, co-exist in the same place and time. But Freud ended his attempt to visualize this multi-dimensional world with the words: 'There is clearly no point in spinning our phantasy any further, for it leads to things that are unimaginable and even absurd.' [SE XXI.70]

There are two photographs of Marie Bonaparte (1882-1962) in the study. This unusual woman left her mark in this room in other ways as well. A number of the antiquities – for example, the large Greek krater standing opposite Freud's bust, the small bronze Venus and the large standing Tang figures on the desk – were her gifts.

In his diary Freud refers to her as 'Princess', for she was not only a direct descendent of Napoleon's younger brother Lucien but also the wife of Prince George of Greece. Consequently she was related to the royal families of Denmark, Russia and England. Too lively and intelligent to be satisfied by the duties associated with her status, she was to find a career and a passion in psychoanalysis.

In 1925 she entered analysis with Freud in Vienna and trained as a psychoanalyst. She went on to become a key figure in both the French Psychoanalytical Society and the international

Marie Bonaparte

Freud arriving in Paris on 5 June 1938 where he was met by Marie Bonaparte and William Bullitt, the American Ambassador to France

psychoanalytical movement. Criminal psychopathology fascinated her and she published a book on a woman who had murdered her pregnant daughter-in-law, *Le Cas de Madame Lefebvre*, and a psychoanalytical study of Edgar Allen Poe whom she termed 'one of the darkest minds there has ever been'.

During the 1930s she was a frequent and welcome guest in Vienna and became one of Freud's closest friends. At the time of the Nazi Anschluss she immediately flew to his aid. Her connections and considerable financial resources helped secure the Freud family's safe passage from Vienna to London.

Martin Freud wrote: '...she had most of father's chief characteristics – his courage, his sincerity, his essential goodness and kindliness and his inflexible devotion to scientific truth. In this sense the similarity of character was almost startling.'

Yvette Guilbert

Yvette Guilbert (1865-1944), the renowned singer and *'diseuse'* made her name as a *café-concert* performer in Paris. A star of the Belle Époque, she was immortalised several times by Toulouse-Lautrec. Freud's collection contains an original lithograph of her. He had first seen her perform in Paris in the 1880s, but did not meet her until the 1920s, through her niece Eva Rosenfeld who was a close friend of Anna Freud and a collaborator at the Burlingham-Rosenfeld school in Vienna. During the 1930s her annual perform-

ances in Vienna were the only theatrical events he attended. She sang in a variety of personae, from schoolgirls to prostitutes. In a letter to her on 8 March 1931, Freud put forward a hypothesis to explain the psychology of the actor: 'repressed desires and traits that have not had the chance to develop are employed to represent the chosen character.' She was intrigued, though not to the extent of entering psychoanalysis.

The signed and dedicated photograph in Freud's study dates from her visit to Maresfield Gardens in 1939, at the time when she gave three recitals at the Wigmore Hall in London. Freud's fondness for her is conveyed by his urging her not to wait until his birthday to come to see him in England: 'At my age every postponement has a painful connotation.'

The glamorous woman in furs whose photograph hangs from the bookshelves of the study was Lou Andreas-Salomé (1861-1937). Born in St Petersburg where her father was a general in the Russian army, she grew up determined to live her own life independently and according to her own convictions. This led first to a platonic *ménage à trois* with Paul Rée and Friedrich Nietzsche, and later to a series of lovers, among them Rainer Maria Rilke. Her marriage with the Professor of Oriental Languages at Göttingen University, F.C. Andreas, was a rational union: she resisted domesticity and pursued her own writing career.

Lou Andreas-Salomé

She was fifty by the time she discovered psychoanalysis and had already established herself as a novelist, poet and critic. Such was her reputation that Freud announced it was 'an honour when she joined the ranks of our collaborators'. He was captivated by her charm and even gave her 'permission' to attend both the meetings of the Vienna Psychoanalytic Society and Alfred Adler's rival discussions, until she could decide where her choice lay. It was unequivocally psychoanalysis which was to dominate the final decades of her life and for her the intellectual and personal aspects of this commitment were inseparable. When she wrote a tribute entitled *My Thanks to Freud*, he urged her to change the word 'Freud' to 'Psychoanalysis' but she refused.

Like many of the early psychoanalysts, she underwent no formal training, but later she was to discuss her cases in detail in her correspondence with Freud and with Anna, to whom she became a close friend and confidante.

Gradiva

The *bas-relief* of a young woman that hangs at the entrance to the study is a plaster-cast of a Roman sculpture from the Vatican Museum. In September 1907 Freud wrote from Rome to his wife that he had recognized a 'familiar, dear face' there. Later he acquired this copy of the figure of a striding woman. The face was

familiar because in 1906 he had written *Delusions and Dreams in Jensens 'Gradiva'*, a study of a short novel, *Gradiva: Ein pompejanisches Phantasiestück*, published in 1903 by Wilhelm Jensen (1837-1911). A copy of Jensen's book containing numerous annotations is now in Freud's library; the relief is also depicted on its cover and plays a vital role in the story.

Freud's *Gradiva* was the first full-length application of psychoanalysis to a literary text. Jensen's hero is an archaeologist who has fallen in love with the figure of the woman on the *bas-relief* and has the delusion of meeting her in real life in Pompeii. But she turns out to be his childhood sweetheart. As Freud shows, his fantasies 'were not capricious products of his imagination, but determined, without his knowing it, by the store of childhood impressions which he had forgotten, but which were still at work in him'.

Jensen's *Gradiva* not only offers an extended metaphor of childhood memories and archaeological relics, it also presents an analogy to the psychoanalytic cure of neurotic obsession, for the book's Gradiva figure enters into the hero's delusion in order to guide him back to reality.

The small print of Ingres' *Oedipus and the Sphinx* on the far wall of the study dramatically highlights the figure of the hero confronting his fate. But the dark background of the picture also resonates in Freud's work. The encounter takes place in a rocky defile and it is a narrow track like this which serves as a structuring metaphor for the first three chapters of *The Interpretation of Dreams*. As he wrote to Fliess on 6 August, 1899:

Ingres' Oedipus

> The whole thing is planned on the model of an imaginary walk. First comes the dark wood of the authorities (who cannot see the trees), where there is no clear view and it is easy to go astray. Then there is a concealed defile through which I lead my readers – my specimen dream with its peculiarities, its details, its indiscretions and its bad jokes – and then all at once, the high ground and the open prospect and the question: 'Which way do you want to go?'

The image contains a sense of constriction followed by expansion, and of tension followed by release. In this process something creative happens, something is moved forward which had seemed blocked. This evokes Freud's early 'pressure technique' in which

Freud's print of Ingres'
Oedipus and the Sphinx
in the Louvre

he applied pressure to the head of his patients and expected, on the release of pressure, an idea or memory to pop into their minds. The memories were detaching themselves from the 'complicated and multi-dimensional organisation' of the pathogenic material, and passing one at a time through the narrow 'defile of consciousness'. 'The whole spatially-extended mass of psychogenic material is in this way drawn through a narrow cleft and thus arrives in consciousness cut up, as it were, into pieces or strips. It is the psychotherapist's business to put these together once more into the organisation which he presumes to have existed.' [SE II:291].

As we enter the study we notice a print of Leonardo da Vinci's cartoon of the *Virgin and Child with St Anne and John the Baptist* hanging next to the bookshelves opposite. The actual cartoon now hangs in the National Gallery, London: the painting of another version is in the Louvre. Freud acquired the print in London, but he already had a smaller photograph of the painting, probably from Paris in 1910. In that year he published his paper 'Leonardo da Vinci and a Memory of his Childhood'. This was Freud's only attempt at a psychoanalytical biography.

Two questions prompted his work. Firstly, why the figures of Mary and her mother, St Anne, fuse together and appear to be the

Leonardo's *Virgin and Child*

same age? And secondly, what is the cause of the smile that characterizes Leonardo's models and is best known in the Mona Lisa? In their respective responses to that question both Walter Pater (by implication) and Marcel Duchamp (explicitly) assign a sexual motive to the sitter's expression. But Freud was less interested in the model than in the artist and his motives. He traces the 'dreamlike fusion' of the dual mother figures back to Leonardo's infantile memories of his own true mother and his stepmother. He suggests that Mona Lisa's smile aroused in the adult Leonardo the two aspects of motherhood he had experienced and which he reproduced in the painting – tenderness and menace. That ambivalent image of the mother was to become one of the foundations of Melanie Klein's work.

Freud's background reading for this study is to be found on the shelves of the library. The main sources are a much-annotated copy of a German translation of the Russian Dmitri Merezhkovski's novel about Leonardo and biographical studies of the artist by Scognamiglio, Solmi and others. From a faulty translation in Merezhkovski's novel, Freud had adopted the mistaken version of Leonardo's memory of a vulture (instead of a kite) touching his lips in infancy. This resulted in an unfounded linking of motherhood and the vulture of Egyptian mythology, the goddess Mut whose name meant mother. On the other hand, Freud's overall interpretation of the painting has been accepted even by such non-Freudian art critics as Kenneth Clark, since it offers plausible clues to otherwise enigmatic aspects of Leonardo's art.

The collection

Greek vases in the study

FREUD'S COLLECTION fills the study and front room. These antiquities created an extraordinary interior work space which was even to survive the move to another country. Today's visitors to the study in London are often astonished to see that Freud worked in a museum of his own creation. So were his patients during his lifetime. In the account of her analysis with Freud, the American poet Hilda Doolittle (H.D.) described him as 'like a curator in a museum surrounded by his priceless collection of Greek, Egyptian and Chinese treasures'. This rich environment was a source of inspiration to his work and a consolation through the trials of his life, particularly the painful deprivations of old age. Like an archaeological site, it is a place where different layers of time are exposed to view. The writer in this study has world history and culture at his fingertips.

The nature of Freud's collecting is hard to define. The collection itself is eclectic and reflects the taste of someone more concerned to accumulate objects with meaning for him than to acquire items which would be impressive to a small band of fellow collectors. The collection is variable in quality; it ranges from pieces which would be given an honoured place in a national museum to even a few fakes. It is not unusual to find fakes in a collection of this time. And some of the Egyptian fakes, it should be added, are of excellent quality. The collection includes terracotta Tang figures which were flooding onto the antiquities market in Europe in the 1920s and '30s, becoming so popular and highly valued that they were extensively copied.

The more we discover about the collection as it is being catalogued by experts, the more it becomes clear that Freud made many very well-considered purchases. We know that he was keen to seek expert advice before making purchases and he was fortunate to have close friends who could advise him. His school friend Emanuel Löwy was professor of archaeology in Rome between 1889 and 1915. Each year he returned to Vienna and on each occasion visited Freud and inspected his new purchases. Many of his publications are in Freud's library. Closer to home was Ernst Kris, an art historian married to Marianne, the daughter of Freud's friend and medical colleague, Oscar Rie. Kris was a pupil of Löwy and an expert on Renaissance gold, cameos and engraved gems. He was a curator at the Vienna Kunsthistorisches Museum and eventually became a psychoanalyst. Robert Lustig, one of the dealers in Vienna from whom Freud regularly made purchases, recalled that Freud would ask him to obtain authentication notes from the curators at the Vienna Kunsthistorisches Museum. Freud also took items there, to Dr Hans Demel, director of the Egyptian and Oriental collection, and to Dr Julius Banko, director of the Antiquities collection, who examined the Greek and Roman material, and a number of these notes survive in the archives of the Freud Museum.

Evidence of when and where Freud acquired his pieces is sporadic because no systematic record of purchases has survived. The majority came through dealers in Vienna, or occasionally from

Paris or Rome. Numerous objects were bought during his travels. Ernest Jones recounts that Freud made a detailed list of his collection in 1914, the same year that Max Pollak made his dramatic etching of Freud at his desk, which is lined with rows of favourite objects. In this scene we can see the splendid white marble statue of the baboon of the Egyptian god Thoth, which still stands at the

edge of the desk. Other pieces still to be found on the desk are the stylised bronze figure of a warrior from Umbria and the tall striding figure of the Egyptian creator goddess Neith. This visual evidence is invaluable since the list Freud compiled is now lost.

Authentication document by Dr Julius Banko for an Athenian red-figured hydria depicting Oedipus and the Sphinx

Despite the voluminous quantity of Freud's correspondence there are relatively few references to the antiquities, but we do know that friends, colleagues and analysands sometimes gave them, and sometimes received them as presents. In 1930 Freud received the Goethe Prize, an award of 10,000 Reichsmarks. Over the next two years or so he was to use part of that money to purchase antiquities, including a painted mummy portrait from the collection of Theodor Graf and a fine Tang figure of a female rider. During the years 1929 to 1939 the *Brief Chronicle* provides a source of references to the collection. The laconic nature of the entries means that not all of the items mentioned can be safely identified but often visitor and gift are noted together. Only three weeks after the arrival in England, for instance, we find such notes as '23rd June 1938 Princess – Cypriot head' or '25th June 1938 Mrs. Gunn with Egypt. antiq.' .

It was in the 1907 edition of *The Psychopathology of Everyday Life* that Freud publicly revealed his passion for collecting. He wrote that an 'irritating and laughable misreading' to which he fell prey when on holiday led him to read as 'Antiquities' every shop sign that in any way resembled that word. Freud concludes that this slip 'betrays the questing spirit of the collector'.

His letters had already given earlier hints of the urge to be a collector of antiquities and curator of his own museum. In 1885, as a young researcher, he attended a dinner at the house of the illustrious Charcot in Paris. A letter described the scene to his fiancée – the furniture, carpets, tapestries, Indian and Chinese antiques. It was 'in short – like a museum'. Here was a model the penniless student could only admire and envy. But by 1896 his earnings were increasing and in that year he mentioned decorating his study with plaster casts. In 1898 he wrote of buying a Roman figure, which his three-year-old daughter Anna called an 'old child'. On 1 August 1899, while he was writing *The Interpretation of Dreams*, he wrote to Fliess of 'old and grubby gods' that took part in the work as paperweights. Two years later, on 8 May 1901, he wrote to him that 'a fragment of Pompeian wall with a centaur and a faun transports me to my longed-for Italy'. By 1909 a collection existed, but it was still in its initial stages. By 1939, however, Freud had amassed over 2000 objects and the collection encompassed items from the ancient Near East, Egypt, Greece, Rome and China, together with a sprinkling of objects which might be described as ethnographic.

Freud never analyzed his own passion for collecting. But his references in letters reveal some interesting associations, particularly childhood and gods, longing and Italy. Desire for travel and love of the classical world were part of the impetus that led to archaeology and collecting antiquities. Freud was a passionate traveller: in fact, there was something exhausting as well as exhaustive about his methodical tourism. Before coming to any new town he would study the places of interest in his Baedeker and however little time he had there, he would try to cram in as many of these as possible. His travelling companions could seldom keep up the pace. The collection is another expression of this voracious desire to possess or re-possess foreign places and past cultures, above all those of the Mediterranean world.

From the beginning, archaeology provided a key metaphor for the emerging techniques and theories of psychoanalysis. To the Wolf Man he said: 'The psychoanalyst like the archaeologist in his excavations must uncover layer after layer of the patient's psyche

Group of Egyptian
shabtis

before coming to the deepest most valuable treasures.' The idea of hidden treasure connects the discoveries of archaeology with the hidden continuity of childhood. One of Freud's early heroes was Heinrich Schliemann, the German merchant who overcame opposition and hostility to excavate Troy, which had previously been regarded as a purely mythical city. Freud wrote to Fliess about him on 28 May 1899: 'The man was happy when he found Priam's treasure, because happiness comes only with the fulfillment of a childhood wish.'

On closer examination we find a series of interesting groups of antiquities in Freud's collection, many of them indicating a very real interest in the aesthetics of objects. The biographer Ernest Jones states that both Kris and Ernst Freud claimed that Freud had 'little aesthetic appreciation'. This may be true of his approach to contemporary paintings and drawings, but his collections of ancient glass and indeed Chinese jade show a considerable interest in the form, colour and shape of objects. In one of the show-cases

In July 1938 Freud's collection had still not been sent on from Vienna and only the terracotta figures given to him in Paris by Marie Bonaparte stand on his desk in London

by the front window there are beautiful pieces of Egyptian, Phoenician, Greek, Roman and Islamic glass, displaying a rich variety of colours and shapes.

Pieces of high quality are found in several areas of the collection. The prehistoric items, including pots and a hand-axe from pre-Dynastic Egypt, are indications of Freud's interest in the earliest origins of human cultures. Like many collections of the time, Freud's has a number of Assyrian and Babylonian cylinder seals, some of which are finely cut. The bronze statues of Egyptian gods and goddesses clustered on his desk are of excellent quality. There is a splendid selection of Egyptian *shabtis*. The groups of Greek vases, whether the pre-classical Corinthian alabastra and aryballoi or the Classical lekythoi, have been carefully selected and show a considered interest. Terracotta figures predominate in one of the cases, including Freud's collection of Erotes, and among them are some delicately modelled figures from the famous cache found at Myrina in Asia Minor. Another case contains a variety of small bronzes, figures of Roman gods and goddesses, miniature stylised Etruscan figures of soldiers, Roman steelyard weights, Egyptian and Etruscan mirrors. The collection also includes a number of small items – amulets, scarabs, engraved gems and beads. In short, the whole makes a cornucopia reflecting Freud's passionate interest in ancient civilisations and 'the questing spirit of the collector'.

The drawers of Freud's desk in London also contain some touching mementos such as his wedding ring, notepaper printed with his two London addresses (Elsworthy Road and Maresfield Gardens), some small Egyptian amulets, a magnifying glass and calipers for measuring small objects. The last two items remind us of the practical side of collecting and of the fact that it gave an old and ill man an intensely fascinating hobby, and access to distant lands, ancient civilizations, religions and mythologies.

On many of the bronze, stone and terracotta items are numbers painted in red. It is clear that the numbers were assigned retrospectively, perhaps for the valuation required by the Nazis, rather than at the time they became part of the collection. This evidence suggests that they were added during the anxious period of April and May of 1938 while the Freuds waited for their emigration papers to arrive. One object that demonstrates this very clearly is a stone Osiris figure now on Freud's desk: this substantial item is mentioned in Freud's *Brief Chronicle* as a gift from his brother Alexander in March 1936. It carries the number 8. This must refer to its position on the desk, as eighth figure on the back row.

In May 1938 a valuation was formally carried out by Hans Demel of the Kunsthistorisches Museum. Freud suspected the Nazi authorities would seize his entire collection. But two days after Demel's visit Freud wrote to his sister-in-law, Minna Bernays: 'The one good piece of news is that my collection has been released. Not a single seizure, only a small payment of 400 Reichmarks. Director Demel of the Museum was very merciful, he assessed it all at only 30,000 RM but that leaves us far below the tax limit for refugees. The removers can begin packing without delay.'

Before all their possessions could be released the Freuds had to pay the tax the Nazis extorted from those they drove into exile: the *Reichsfluchtsteuer* amounted to 31,329 RM or 25 per cent of Freud's estimated taxable assets. But because their financial assets had been seized, to pay such a sum was impossible. Once again the Princess was to play a central role in the drama of the emigration when she advanced the required tax.

On the journey to their temporary home in London in June 1938 Marie Bonaparte showed her great solicitude for Freud's well-being by presenting him with some terracotta figures as a consolation for the absence of the collection, which was still in storage in Vienna. In August the collection finally arrived in England. Two months later Freud moved into Maresfield Gardens which had been prepared by Martha and Paula Fichtl, and he was once more surrounded by the familiar furniture and rugs. From his desk he could look through the French windows to the garden, and arranged around the room were five vitrines filled with the precious collection. The antiquities also spilled over onto the tops of cupboards, shelves, and the mantelpiece, and framed fragments of wall painting were hung on the walls.

Since 1989 exhibitions of objects have travelled to the USA, Japan, Brazil, Belgium, the Netherlands, Austria, Mexico, Italy, Portugal, France Germany and Australia. For all of these exhibitions catalogues have been produced, each time bringing to light some new discovery about one or other of the objects. The catalogues attract the interest of specialists from around the world: stage by stage we gain greater insight into Freud's collection. His own favourite metaphor of the careful uncovering of the layers of the unconscious by the psychoanalyst might well also be applied to our 'excavation' of his treasured antiquities.

Athena

This small bronze statuette is Roman, 1st or 2nd century AD, after a Greek original of the 5th century BC. The poet H.D. wrote about it after she arrived in Vienna to begin her analysis with Freud in 1933. He remarked that she was the first of his patients who had looked at his collection before looking at him. Gratified by their shared interest in antiquities, he proudly showed her this figure, saying, 'She is perfect, only she has lost her spear.'

At that time the figure occupied pride of place in the centre of his writing desk. Though Athena was the goddess of wisdom and war, she also had the reputation of coming to the aid of her heroes. Indeed, she became the mascot for the emigration to England. Before Freud knew he would be able to export his collection, he gave this figure to Princess Marie Bonaparte to smuggle out on his behalf, collecting it in Paris en route to London. 'We left proud and rich under the protection of Athene,' he wrote to her from England.

Amulets

Amulets, magic talismans or charms, produced in every culture throughout history, were worn to endow the wearer with magical powers, or to invoke protection, possibly from a god or goddess. They bear witness to the belief systems of ancient cultures. Freud possessed a considerable collection of amulets, the majority from ancient Egypt. Many were associated with funerary rites and were produced in a profusion of shapes, sizes and materials.

Only a small selection of his collection is shown but it illustrates the extent of his interest in these talismans. The fine bronze *aegis* of the lion-headed goddess Sahkmet still has remnants of glass inlays. Among her attributes Sahkmet represented the great heat of the sun, and had the power to destroy the enemies of the sun god. Not an amulet intended for personal use, the *aegis* would have been offered as a gift in a shrine to provide protection.

Osiris, Egyptian god of the dead, is represented in a number of amulets, also intended to give protection. One of the symbols associated with Osiris, the *djed*-pillar, possibly represented the backbone of the god. Invocations spoken over the *djed*-pillar were part of the ritual of the *Book of the Dead*. Wallis Budge's translation and commentary on this ancient text is in Freud's library. He also possessed two fragments of Egyptian linen mummy bandage inscribed with excerpts from the book. One of the most popular protective amulets, the eye of Horus, is associated with the falcon-headed god, son of Osiris and Isis. Also known as the *wedjat* or *udjat*-eye, literally translated as 'the sound one', it contained healing properties as well as being a powerful protector. It represented the eye of Horus, wounded by his evil brother Seth, which was healed by the god Thoth.

Phallic amulets to enhance potency or fertility are found in many cultures. Freud's collection contains over twenty examples which come from Egypt, Rome, Etruria and Japan and are made of Egyptian faience, bronze and ivory.

The hundreds of amulets in the collection show Freud's interest in magical objects and religious beliefs. A sentence from *The Psychopathology of Everyday Life* explains this interest: 'I believe that a large part of the mythological view of the world, which extends a long way into most modern religions, *is nothing but psychology projected into the external world.*'[SE VI.258] The religious and superstitious see unconscious factors mirrored in 'supernatural reality': psychoanalysis reinterprets their beliefs as the psychology of the unconscious.

Aegean collection

Freud's collection of Aegean antiquities was select and well-chosen; it seems likely that Emanuel Löwy was the guiding influence in their purchase. Löwy had a particular interest in pre-Classical Crete and Greece and taught courses on Mycenaean and Archaic Greece after his appointment to a professorship in Rome. The coincidence of interests of the two friends must have made the collection of Aegean material particularly enjoyable for Freud.

He acquired nineteen pieces in all. Perhaps the most beautiful is one of the three Mycenaean stirrup jars, which belong to the period of their great palaces, and are of a type that may well have been excavated by Heinrich Schliemann who pioneered the Mycenean excavations. These pieces clearly indicate that Freud took a close interest in the archaeological developments of his time.

Bodhisattvas and Buddhas

In 1909 Freud visited Tiffany in New York where he purchased a bronze bust of the Buddha, probably the first Buddhist object he acquired. Although there are relatively few Buddhist items in his collection, their quality and interest is exceptional.

Two ivory Buddhas are particularly fine. Both are Burmese from the borders with Thailand. One is a seated, earth-touching Buddha, the other depicts the penitent Buddha walking, and is a rare representation of the figure in movement. Freud refers to one of them in his diary on 7 May 1934, the day after his birthday, so perhaps it was a gift to himself.

In *Beyond the Pleasure Principle* (1920) Freud introduced the notion of the death instinct, relating it to what the analyst Barbara Low had termed the 'Nirvana Principle'. But in Freud the Buddhist reference bears no hint of enlightenment: it refers only to the tendency of living substance to revert to its inorganic origins. The Buddha figures which represent this 'speculation' also reverse that trend towards death. Although immobile, they are infused with life and love by their owners and observers.

The gods of ancient Egypt entered the dreams of the young Sigmund Freud, as we know from his own account in *The Interpretation of Dreams*. Small figures of the Egyptian gods inhabited his collection, and his desk in particular. By the end of his life Freud had acquired a series of fine statuettes representing many of the major gods and goddesses from the extensive Egyptian pantheon. These are largely small bronzes which worshippers may have presented as donations to the gods at temples and shrines or used for private devotion; most date from the Late Period, 716-332 BC. These finely modelled figures vividly evoke the complex and colourful myths of Egypt and demonstrate how cults developed and grew over millennia. As myths became entwined, the gods acquired new attributes. The elegant seated figure of Isis, sister-wife of Osiris, shows the goddess wearing a headdress surmounted by the horned disc also associated with the cow goddess Hathor. Osiris, a god whose myth grew ever more complex through time, is to be found in a number of representations in Freud's collection. On the desk are a fine head and a small figure which still displays fragments of its original silvering. Though Freud never travelled to Egypt, through his library and collection, he could visit the ancient sites in his mind's eye.

Egyptian gods and goddesses

Eros

In early Greek mythology Eros represented a primeval force. Only later was his image sentimentalized. In Freudian theory the fundamental drive, the instinct that strives for union, corresponds to the early Eros. It is the representation of sexuality seen as the driving force of animal life and termed 'libido'.

Of the several Eros figures in the collection, the largest and most elegant is the Eros from Myrina, a terracotta of the 2nd century BC. Freud recorded its acquisition on 5 September 1934. It is likely that its empty hands once held a lyre.

Presents received and given were one of the great pleasures of the
Freud household. In 1919 Anna Freud wrote to her brother Ernst
asking him to help her find a birthday present for their father. She
suggested that he should 'look around for jade in Munich… at
least I would like to have something especially beautiful for him
this year'.

Freud mentions the purchase of jade in his *Brief Chronicle*,
sometimes as an addition for his collection, but also as presents for
his friends and family. Two items are noteworthy, both Chinese.
One is a triple vase fashioned in the form of the 'Three Friends in
Winter'. These are three trees imbued with a rich symbolism for
the Chinese – the plum tree, pine and bamboo. The plum represents
independence, flowering at a time when little else is growing. The
pine survives the winter, it represents endurance and the constancy
of friendship in adversity. Bamboo is renowned for durability, it
bends but does not break: it is symbolic of the scholar and gentle-
man and one who remains loyal. This vase might have been a

Jade

Jade triple vase

present to Freud from one of his family or friends, symbolising attributes he represented for them.

When Freud gave Anna a sumptuous pin of two jade discs with sinuous gold dragons entwined in them he wrote an 'authentication' note to accompany it. It read 'Chinese jewellery (previous century) both plates connected by a needle can be parted and used separately. The ornamentation is fine gold. On 3 Dec. 1933 Love Papa'.

Rugs

Freud's study and consulting room as arranged in both Vienna and London display an opulence which is quite remarkable, even extraordinary – quite unlike the utilitarian furnishings of most present-day doctors' and psychoanalysts' offices. This opulence is created largely by the glowing colours and rich textures of the oriental rugs on the floors, draped on the couch and over the furniture. Freud's collection is of very fine quality and it is possible that he may have obtained at least part of his collection from his brother-in-law, Moritz Freud, an importer of carpets who was married to his sister Mitzi. Vienna, so close to the western-most boundary of the Ottoman empire, has always been a flourishing centre for the trade in oriental carpets. This trade, and the nineteenth-century taste for orientalising decor, developed the fashion for the lavish use of oriental carpets and rugs.

Perhaps the best-known rug in the collection covers the famous psychoanalytic couch. With a thick pile coloured in deep red and blues, it transforms the plain and simple couch into a fitting landscape for the retelling of dreams. It was woven by one of the tribes of the Qashqa'i Confederacy whose territories extend through the west of Iran. The rug is decorated with traditional patterns: bold geometric shapes are filled with stylised plants, deer and peacocks. At the foot of the couch is a table covered with a rug of a deep russet red. Regarded as the finest piece in the collection, it is an *asmalyk* – a five-sided rug which was one of a pair intended to cover both sides of the leading camel in a wedding procession – woven by a Turkoman tribe, the Tekke nomads who range from the Caspian Sea as far as Afghanistan. The wool has a fine silky texture, and the pattern constructed from the shapes of stylised birds occurs only rarely. Although Freud's collection of antiquities attracts most interest from scholars and the public, the rugs which enrich the study demonstrate that Freud also had an eye for quality and beauty in textiles.

**Turkoman *asmalyk*
covering a small table
in the study**

The library

A HOUSE REFLECTS ITS OWNER. Above all the library, for it contains the traces of the owner's work, pleasures and intellectual environment. Freud's study is a perspective on another world and time. The writing-desk and couch, the crowded bookshelves and the antiquities displayed in glass cases between the books – all are aspects of Freud's life. Each of them mirrors a different facet of his world and his mind.

The other world of his library is the culture that created psychoanalysis. Some of the books, such as the works of Charles Darwin and Thomas Huxley and other early scientific mentors, or the English empirical philosophers that his university teacher Franz Brentano recommended, such as Locke, were acquired as early as the 1870s during his student years. From his years as a medical student, Freud also retained medical and scientific texts by Theodor Meynert, Gilles de la Tourette, Helmholtz, Brücke, Kraepelin and Mach. There are also anatomical textbooks and studies in physiology and neurology from his pre-analytic days. In fact, we can follow Freud's scientific career from the books he studied and from his own neurological publications: on eels and petromyzon; on a new gold-staining technique for microscopy; on the properties of cocaine; on infantile hemiplegia. Among his other early work we find *On Aphasia*, his first full-length book, in which he discussed the localization of speech functions, a key issue in neuropsychology since it pinpoints the problem of links between mind and brain.

Of the nineteenth century pioneers who created the atmosphere from which a scientific psychology emerged, Gustav Fechner is among the most notable for his speculations on 'psychophysics' and the role of dreams and imagination in mental life. Such books were whetstones for Freud's thought. Other catalysts or antagonists are to be found, for example, in Rudolf Meringer and Karl Mayer's psycho-linguistic study of slips of the tongue and misreadings, published in 1895, six years before *The Psychopathology of Everyday Life*. In the same class are the popular linguistic studies of Rudolf Kleinpaul, which provided useful material on words and symbols for *The Interpretation of Dreams*. The early sexologists are on these shelves too: Havelock Ellis, Krafft-Ebing, Moll, Bloch and Bölsche, whose observations prompted or corroborated Freud's thoughts on sexual development and the role of childhood sexuality.

The extraordinary range of Freud's thought and writing is well-known, but still there are surprises. His first book publication, for instance, is on the shelves – a translation into German of three articles by the nineteenth century British philosopher John Stuart Mill (*Grote's Plato, Thornton on Labour and its Claims* and *Chapters on Socialism*), and one by Harriet Taylor Mill (*Enfranchisement of Women*). It was done for

Wooden Egyptian mummy masks in the library

money in 1879, at the request of the editor Theodor Gomperz, whose *Greek Thinkers* Freud was later to place among his 'ten good books'. There are some other of his translations here too – of Charcot, for example, done in 1886, as an act of homage to a respected teacher – and the last of all, Princess Marie Bonaparte's book about her chow, Topsy, which Freud translated (in this case partly as a token of friendship), together with his daughter Anna in 1938-39.

During his lifetime Freud's study and consulting rooms came to look more and more like a museum as the collection he had begun in the 1890s gradually grew. But as a living workshop it was never static, and nowadays its final form is like an archaeological site with its exposed strata revealing different layers of activity. In this respect, too, the study reflects the thought it produced, for Freud's fascination with the ancient world and classical cultures preceded his psychological work. He told Stefan Zweig that he had read more archaeology than psychology and a large part of the library is devoted to the ancient world. Classical Rome, Greece and Ancient Egypt are represented by an almost professional archaeological collection of beautifully bound and illustrated volumes, including excavation reports, histories and encyclopaedias. The daily life of the ancient world is represented as much in the books as in the showcases of antiquities they frame, or in the prints of Rome and Egypt on the walls. Freud grew up, and lived with, the idea of Egypt, Greece and Rome as cultural prototypes.

Archaeologists – those who bring to light lost cultures – have a place of honour in the library. Layard of Nineveh and

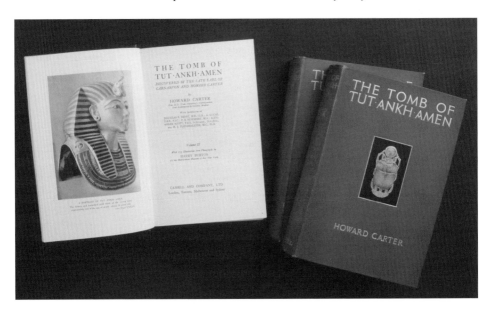

Egyptologists such as Wallis Budge, Flinders Petrie and Gaston Maspero are here and, of course, Heinrich Schliemann too. His *Tiryns* and *Mykenae* are on the shelves, and his *Ilios* was a present Freud gave to himself in May 1899. Freud also possessed guides to the Assyrian and Egyptian languages, to hieroglyphs and cuneiform inscriptions. It was through his books that he vicariously participated in archaeological excavations: with Arthur Evans at Knossos, Leonard Woolley in Ur of the Chaldees or Howard Carter in his world-famous discovery of the tomb of Tutankhamun. In his final years he was hoping that excavations at El Amarna might unearth some discovery which would corroborate his hypotheses on the development of religion in *Moses and Monotheism*.

Freud's study illustrates the evolution of psychoanalysis in four dimensions. Layers of time underlie the visible space containing desk, collection and couch; the library books correspond to shards that situate a particular development. For example, we can follow the background reading for *Moses and Monotheism*. A section of the historical books is concerned with the origins of religion and myth, and particularly with the figure of Moses and the Jewish religion. It is clear that Freud's ideas on Moses were influenced by Breasted's discussions of the Egyptian Pharaoh Akhnaton, the founder of a short-lived, apparently monotheistic religion. And there are also Judaica, such as the Babylonian Talmud and the Jewish Encyclopaedia – books which may have nurtured his preoccupation with the origins of Judaism.

Historical reference works to the ancient world include the invaluable Cambridge Ancient History and there is also a Cambridge Medieval History. Modern works, however, are less numerous: these include such classics as Motley's *The Rise of the Dutch Republic* and Lord Macaulay's *History of England*. Macaulay's *Speeches* and his *Critical and Historical Essays* are also evidence of an early enthusiasm for this writer, one that implies a sympathy for his liberal politics and for the English puritan revolution which he extolled. (Indeed, one of Freud's sons was named Oliver in honour of Cromwell.) The Dutch writer 'Multatuli' (Edward Douwes Dekker) whose letters and novels are in the library was another favourite and it is likely that Freud approved of his anti-imperialism and his progressive views, on sexual education, for example.

The library makes visible the place of literature in Freud's life and work. If archaeology and history provide a model for individual development, literature provides the actual cases, the experiments in practical psychology and the raw material for the experience of being human. Freud considered that *Dichter* (the German for 'poet' or 'creative writer' in general) had intuitively gained the insights which psychoanalysis laboured to systematize and study scientifically. His reading of novels or poetry usually involved a level beyond simple pleasure, namely the urge to understand and explain its effect. He discussed literary effects in his work, in his correspondence and often face to face with the many writers he knew.

One of the first of the *Dichter* to attract psychoanalytic inter-pretation, during the 1890s in Freud's letters to his friend Wilhelm Fliess, was Conrad Ferdinand Meyer, and his works remain in the collection. Sometimes literary merit, or its lack, were of less inter-est to Freud than the psychological content of the work: Wilhelm Jensen's novel *Gradiva* is one example: this book contains an unu-

sual number of annotations, for Freud was not a habitual or pro-
fuse annotator. His marginal markings are often notes towards a
publication he was working on, rather than a reader's first reac-
tions. Books he is known to have loved and respected generally
remain unmarked. There are, for example, numerous annotations
in Schreber's *Memoirs of my Nervous Illness,* which was to be the
basis of the first psychoanalytic study of paranoia. On the other
hand, Freud's own works are almost entirely unmarked, apart
from a first edition of *The Interpretation of Dreams* which contains
a few emendations, and a first edition of *The Psychopathology of
Everyday Life,* interleaved with blank pages in which he has handwritten a number of additional cases.

Goethe formed an essential element of Freud's cultural
background. The 128-volume complete edition of his works –
entirely unmarked – occupies the entire centre of the wall behind
his desk. Goethe is repeatedly quoted and was the topic of a
paper, *A Childhood Recollection from 'Dichtung und Warheit'* (1917),
which holds a subtext relating to Freud's own infancy. Like
Goethe, Freud too had a younger brother whose death he desired;
Goethe too was his mother's golden boy. Freud's speech in acceptance of the Goethe Prize even cites a case of psychological therapy
in Goethe's own life as a prototypical example of psychoanalytic
methods.

Shakespeare's work in English and in its classic German
translation by Schlegel and Tieck, is also unmarked, but for a copy
of *Macbeth,* where it is not the text but the scholarly apparatus that
has been annotated for use in Freud's paper of 1916: 'Some
Character-Types Met with in Psycho-Analytic Work'. From the
beginning Freud cited Hamlet as evidence for the universality of
the Oedipus complex and also as the first example of the modern
neurotic whose ability to act is 'sicklied o'er with the pale cast of
thought'. Several works relate to the question of Shakespeare's
identity: Freud became convinced that Edward de Vere, 17th Earl
of Oxford, was the true author. Psychoanalysis investigates concealed motives and repressed urges: in his reading of literature
and history, Freud followed the same lines in seeking a concealed
or repressed author.

Heine, whose complete works are here, was a writer who
appealed to Freud for his intelligence, for his political and social
attitudes and for his satires on religion and accepted wisdom.
Among Freud's fellow Viennese the nineteenth-century comic

dramatist Nestroy offered him many examples of pre-Freudian slips. And Arthur Schnitzler wrote cynical studies of erotically-charged social relationships in turn-of-century Vienna which parallelled Freud's own scientific work. The two men were acquainted and in a letter to him Freud addressed him as his own literary alter ego or *Doppelgänger*. There were also writers whom Freud disliked but who provided case histories, for example Dostoevsky, whose *Brothers Karamazov* served as raw material for

Works on archaeology, history and literature in the study. The complete Goethe occupies the centre shelves

Psychoanalytical works, journals and reference books in the front room. In the centre is the Abu Simbel painting which hung over the couch in Vienna

Freud's essay 'Dostoevsky and Parricide' (1928).

The theoretical dialogue of psychoanalysis with literature often took the form of actual encounters, for Freud knew many contemporary writers. He was friends with Stefan and Arnold Zweig and he met and corresponded with Thomas Mann. Dedicated copies of their work are to be found in the front study. He also corresponded with Romain Rolland whose social and political stance he greatly respected. In *The Future of an Illusion* he discusses, from a sceptic's viewpoint, Rolland's 'oceanic feeling' as the basis of religious mysticism. One of Rolland's books in the library, *Liluli*, bears the author's handwritten dedication to Freud: 'Au détructeur d'illusions' ('To the destroyer of illusions'). Many other famous writers also visited him, such as André Breton, Thornton Wilder and H.G. Wells and too many to mention were deeply influenced by his work. On the other hand, the influence of literature on Freud is reflected in the many allusions that not only illustrate psychoanalytic arguments but in some cases actually become a theoretical underpinning.

In his 1926 defence of non-medical psychoanalysis, *The Question of Lay-analysis*, Freud proposed that the training of analysts should be wide-ranging and go beyond medicine. He recommended that depth-psychology be the principal subject, but that biology and the science of sexual life and psychiatric symptomatology should also have a place. But beyond that, the history of civilization, mythology, the psychology of religion and the science of literature were all necessary for the psychoanalyst to understand the clinical material.

This wide curriculum serves as a sketch of the main subject areas contained in Freud's library. As his personal and idiosyncratic collection, it demonstrates the range and depth of his cultural interests out of which his synthesis of psychoanalytic knowledge grew. Psychoanalysis, he maintained, was a scientific enterprise and a 'part of psychology', but at the same time he insisted that it draw its evidence and confirmation not only from the clinical encounter, but also from the entire range of cultural studies. Eventually those other fields of knowledge would in turn be subjected to revaluation through Freud's psychoanalytic discoveries.

The history of Freud's library

The largest remaining part of Freud's personal library is now on display at 20 Maresfield Gardens. In 1938, during the last weeks in Vienna before emigrating, Freud spent some of his time selecting those volumes he wished to bring with him. A selection of his library – over 800 titles – he sold, perhaps to raise ready money. It is not clear upon what basis this selection was made. That collection was bought by the New York State Psychiatric Institute and taken to America, and is now housed in a special collection at Columbia University, New York. The remainder, over 1600 titles plus various offprints and journals, he was able to bring to London where they surrounded him in his study as they had done in Vienna.

Freud lent, gave and exchanged books throughout his life and few of the volumes he is known to have owned early in life have survived. Those still extant represent mainly, but not exclusively, the interests of his mature years. Once psychoanalysis became established and attracted supporters and practitioners Freud received a flow of works, often dedicated, from followers and admirers; he was also often sent unsolicited books by his popularisers. Consequently, some of the library books are found to have uncut pages.

Philippson Bible

'My deep engrossment in the Bible story (almost as soon as I had learnt the art of reading) had, as I recognized much later, an enduring effect upon the direction of my interest,' Freud wrote in *An Autobiographical Study*. The version of the Bible Freud was referring to here was the Old Testament translated and edited by Ludwig Philippson, the first volume of which was published in 1839. It was unusual in that it had not just the Hebrew, but also a German parallel text. Philippson had added an extensive commentary on the life, customs and archaeology of the Ancient World and the work is heavily illustrated. It is interesting that it contains many illustrations of Egyptian gods, the sort of figures Freud later collected. In addition Freud owned a complete second edition of this Bible, perhaps purchased for his research for his book *Moses and Monotheism*.

On his thirty-fifth birthday, Freud's father gave him the rebound fragments of the very Bible which he remembered from his childhood, with a 'Gedenkblatt' or commemorative note which records Freud's birth in 1856 with an inscription: 'as a reminder of love from your father, who loves you with everlasting love' – poignant words, in view of the importance, and ambivalence, of the father-son relationship for Freud.

As for his views on religion, over the course of forty years Freud was to produce a number of different but in many ways interconnected theories. (1) Religion is a 'universal obsessional ritual', designed to avert imaginary misfortunes and control unconscious impulses. (2) Religion is an attempt to master the Oedipus complex. (3) Religion is the return of the repressed. (This is similar to the previous theory, but in this case religion is either working through a trauma from the distant human past, or from the forgotten past of the individual.) (4) Religion is a reaction to infantile helplessness. (5) Religion echoes infantile states of 'bliss', a spirituality equivalent to Romain Rolland's 'oceanic' feeling.

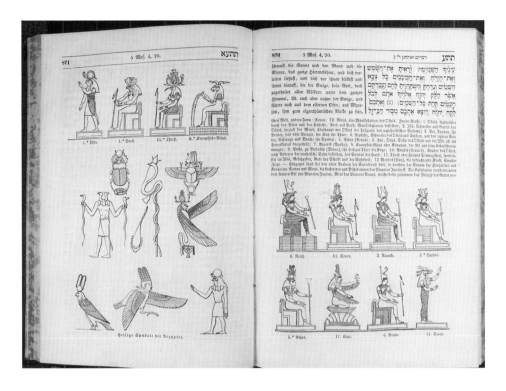

(6) Religion is a mass delusion or a paranoid wish-fulfilment.

(7) Religion is a way to hold groups together.

All of these theories have been criticized as over-simple, but the main objection to them is to the implication that religion is a neurosis. In recent years psychoanalysts and theologians have suggested new approaches to the relationship between psychoanalysis and religion which appreciate the many similarities as well as the differences between them. Freud, however, remained uncompromising. 'The whole thing is so patently infantile, so foreign to reality, that to anyone with a friendly attitude to humanity it is painful to think that the majority of mortals will never be able to rise above this view of life,' he stated in *Civilization and its Discontents* in 1930.

Pages from the family Bible. In *The Interpretation of Dreams* Freud analysed an early anxiety dream of bird-headed figures: 'The strangely draped and unnaturally tall figures with birds' beaks were derived from illustrations to Philippson's Bible.' [SE V. 583]

Early in the century Freud bought, or was given, a scrapbook into which he stuck some of his favourite quotations. He filled only ten pages of the book, but the passages he chose reveal his reading, his tastes and his preoccupations at that period. Theodor Fontane, Goethe, Schiller, Multatuli and Anatole France figure most prominently. Judging from many of the Anatole France quotations, what

The common-place book

appealed to him about this author was his witty debunking of religious faith and commonly-held prejudices. But one of the France quotations can be seen as an example of Freud's search for literary 'alibis' for his ideas: 'What we see at night are the unhappy remains of what we neglected the previous day. Dreams are often the revenge of things one despises or the reproach of abandoned

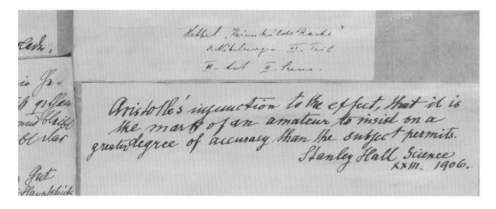

beings' (Anatole France, *Le Lys Rouge*). A different sort of alibi, a response to those who criticized psychoanalysis as unscientific, is seen when he quotes: 'Aristotle's injunction to the effect, that it is the mark of an amateur to insist on a greater degree of accuracy than the subject permits' (Stanley Hall, Science XXIII. 1906).

The Goethe Prize

In August 1930 the city of Frankfurt awarded Freud the prestigious Goethe Prize. Founded in 1927, the two previous winners were Stefan George and Albert Schweitzer. In *An Autobiographical Study* Freud described this award as 'the climax of my life as a citizen'. It signified an official acceptance of psychoanalysis and in addition it conferred 10,000 Reichsmarks which Freud used as a fund to help friends and family members and also to buy himself antiquities.

Because Freud was too ill to travel, his daughter Anna went to Frankfurt to accept the prize on his behalf and deliver his speech of acceptance. In it he defended the attempts of biographers and psychoanalysts to account for the characters of great men. He argued that Goethe himself would not have been hostile to psychoanalysis and that he had in fact himself come to some of its insights, such as the recognition of the primal power of Eros, and had anticipated aspects of its methods, notably the cathartic effect of confession.

Freud's paper 'A Childhood Recollection from *Dichtung und*

> **D**en von ihr gestifteten
>
> ## GOETHEPREIS
>
> verleiht in diesem Jahre die
>
> ## STADT FRANKFURT
>
> dem als Schöpfer grundlegend neuer Be-
> trachtungsformen anerkannten Forscher
>
> ## SIGMUND FREUD

Wahrheit' depicts Goethe as 'his mother's undisputed darling', just as he himself was, and in a letter to Arnold Zweig about the award Freud wrote: 'The fantasy of a closer relationship with Goethe is all too appealing.' That final phrase epitomised his attraction to the artist and at the same time his sense that his viewpoint and that of psychoanalysis differed from the artist's outlook. 'Our attitude to fathers and teachers is, after all, an ambivalent one since our reverence for them regularly conceals a component of hostile rebellion.' [SE XXI.212]

Archives and research

PSYCHOANALYSIS IS A THEORY concerned with individual history, but in all his writing Freud made only one theoretical reference to archives, which are a traditional basis of history. In 'The Psychical Mechanism of Forgetfulness' (1898) he wrote that 'the function of memory, which we like to regard as an archive, open to anyone who is curious, is... subjected to restriction by a trend of the will' [SE III.297]. This is part of Freud's earliest description of unconscious mechanisms, with the Unconscious itself depicted as a potential resource like an archive. One hundred years later the analogy could be extended, for sources of information have proliferated: archive documentation now includes film, television and video, sound recording and computers.

Though the Freud archive was founded before the appearance of new technology, it includes images and tape recordings, photos and press cuttings as well as documents and letters. The Freud Museum itself opened just at a time when personal computers were becoming widespread. Consequently it was among the earliest museums to set up an electronic database of all its collections. This means that access to material is simpler, responses to queries quicker and organizing data more efficient. Moreover, the London archive continues to grow, not only through donations of papers, photographs and other records relating to the Freuds and the history of psychoanalysis, but also electronically, through databases of letters and works.

The core of the museum archive is the Freud family's correspondence, papers and photo albums. Most of Freud's original manuscripts were deposited in the Sigmund Freud Archive at the Library of Congress in Washington, set up by the New York analyst Dr K. R. Eissler. During Anna Freud's lifetime he collected Freud material and supervised its removal from Maresfield Gardens to Washington. However, photocopies of the material were left in the house. Consequently, the Museum can supplement the collection in Washington and serve as a copy archive for European researchers. In addition to these copies, some of the written material consists of original papers and this collection continues to be increased by donations. Since one aim of the museum is to foster research and public interest in the Freuds and their legacy, the archives remain 'open to anyone who is curious' (the only pre-condition being that researchers make an appointment in advance).

Documents

All his life Freud was a voluminous correspondent. His first preserved letter dates from 1863 when at the age of seven he wrote to his half-brother Emanuel in England; the last from 19 August 1939, a month before his death, to the poet Albrecht Schaeffer. There are long exchanges of letters with friends, beginning with the earliest teenage correspondence with Emil Fluss in 1872. The early letters reveal the emergence of Freud the literary stylist, as well as affording glimpses into the formation of his character. The massive correspondences of his middle years with Fliess, Jung, Ferenczi, Abraham and Eitingon provide essential background to the growth of his ideas and the development of the psycho-analytic movement. Later correspondences from the 1920s and '30s, such as those with Lou Andreas-Salomé or Jeanne Lampl-de Groot, reveal both his capacity for friendship and his growing detachment from analytical politics. His correspondents also included eminent writers as well as doctors and scientific figures: we find Thomas Mann, Rilke, H.G. Wells, Stefan and Arnold Zweig here, as well as such figures as Charcot, Bleuler and Einstein. And the private and domestic sides of his life are revealed in family letters, among them a file dedicated to travel letters sent home from 1900 to 1930. Official documentation includes copies of his birth certificate, his mother's travel pass to Leipzig in 1859 and his various university and military service papers.

Anna Freud's papers cover a similar range, from her early poems to the receipts for medicines prescribed in old age. There is also material belonging to other members of the family. Both Anna and her brother Martin held official posts in the psychoanalytical movement. Since the family's history is so closely connected to that of psychoanalysis in general, a number of files relate to the business of the Vienna Psychoanalytic Society up to its dissolution in 1938, and to its training programmes in the 1920s and '30s. There are, for example, papers and protocols of the Vienna society's training committee during that period. Earlier official papers include statutes, letters and circulars documenting the early years of the International Psychoanalytic Association from its founding in 1910. In all, there are over 10,000 documents.

Some of the historical background to Freud's life is documented in a collection of press cuttings from the 1920s and '30s. They provide a factual record of how he was viewed in his own time, as well as conveying the atmosphere of rumours and fabrications that surrounded him. (On 24 July 1938, for example, the *Sunday Pictorial* informed its readers that Freud had spent the month before emigration mixing poisons. On 28 October 1938 *L'Intransigeant* reported that Freud would be travelling to Hollywood to supervise a film starring Humphrey Bogart and Bette Davis.)

Photographs

The museum inherited a unique fund of images – the Freud family photograph collection which contains around 4,000 photos from the 1860s to the 1980s. This rich visual record of Freud, his family and his colleagues is in constant use as source material for publications, journalism, exhibitions and films.

Although Freud's face has become one of the most familiar of the century, reproduced and caricatured countless times, a fund of unknown photos of him exists, taken of him alone or with family and colleagues. Some record family holidays when the children were still young, others show visits to psychoanalytic congresses. Apart from the official group photos taken on such occasions, we also find private scenes among them, such as Freud and Anna in the streets and cafés of The Hague in 1920. In all, there are over 200 photos featuring Sigmund Freud. Many of the late images of Freud, like the *Home Movies*, show him with the beloved chows.

Some of the photos bear inscriptions or even brief messages and this increases their documentary value. The earliest family album begins with Victorian daguerrotypes of relatives, some of them still unidentified. Unposed holiday shots begin at the turn of the century with the first sights of an unfamiliar, relaxed Freud among his family and children. Anna Freud figures in many of the other earlier photos: later there is also a series documenting her holiday cottage in Hochrotherd during the 1930s, firstly its repair and transformation by her brother Ernst, the architect, then two photo albums with pictures of the cottage and surroundings,

inscribed with little couplets praising the place, written by her as a gift for her father. Later photos from the 1940s to the 1980s document both her private life and the numerous conferences and official functions she attended.

Congress of German Natural Scientists and Doctors in Vienna, 1894. Freud is third from the right in the second row

Her work is also well documented, particularly the Jackson Nursery she set up in Vienna in 1937 and the War Nurseries and Hampstead Clinic she founded in London. The analyst Willi Hoffer recorded many of the games and activities of the children in systematic sequences of pictures. There are over five hundred of these images, many of which are amusing and touching in themselves as well as being of value in the study of child psychology.

The photograph collection also includes a curious medley of old photographic prints of famous sights and paintings. Most are reproductions of old masters such as Giotto, Raphael, Titian, Rembrandt, and so on. There are also tourist scenes, primarily landscapes and cathedrals in Italy, which were probably reminders of holidays spent there around the turn of the century. A few can be directly connected with specific journeys and published work: for example, the Leonardo paintings referred to in Freud's study of da Vinci, the Michelangelo statue of Moses to which he devoted an article, the Etruscan tombs near Orvieto referred to in *The Interpretation of Dreams* and the Signorelli frescoes that feature in *The Psychopathology of Everyday Life*.

Public programme

One of the far-reaching objectives of the Freud Museum is to heighten public awareness of the applications and ramifications of Sigmund Freud's work. Early in its existence the Museum embarked on a lively programme of lectures and conferences that, over the years, has considered such diverse topics as ecology, feminism, horror films, humour, literature, art theory, anthropology, race and racism, nursery education, the psychology of ageing, and even 'psychoanalysis and football' (1998). Some of these conferences broke new ground in the application of psychoanalysis, building bridges with practitioners from other disciplines and professions. Other conferences provided a forum for debates within psychoanalysis itself, such as the problem of case presentations in psychoanalytic discourse, or the current status of 'Hysteria' as a diagnostic category. Freud's 150th anniversary in 2006 provided the opportunity for a major international symposium 'Freud Yesterday/Freud Today'. More recently a conference on 'Psychoanalysis, Fascism and Fundamentalism', co-organised with Middlesex University, has been published in a special issue of the journal *Psychoanalysis and History*.

From the beginning we have been concerned to show the relevance of Freud's work to modern thought and contemporary social life. None of this would have been possible without the generous support of the many individuals and organizations who have given their time and effort to speak at our events, and to those many more who will support us in the future. More information about past conferences is available on the Freud Museum website.

Third International Psychoanalytical Congress at Weimar in 1911. Freud is flanked by Sándor Ferenczi and C.G. Jung

Sigmund Freud 1856-1939: his life and work

On 25th October 1931, at a public ceremony in the town of Freiberg (Příbor) in Moravia, a plaque was unveiled celebrating the birth of Sigmund Freud on 6 May 1856. Freud himself, now seventy-five years old and suffering from cancer of the jaw and heart trouble, was unable to attend; his youngest daughter Anna read his speech of thanks in his place. It concluded with the words: '…deeply buried within me there still lives the happy child of Freiberg, the first-born son of a youthful mother, who received his first indelible impressions from this air, from this soil.'[1] Freud's family left Freiberg in 1859, the year Darwin published *The Origin of Species*. They travelled first to Leipzig, then on to Vienna. During his self-analysis of the 1890s, Freud was to unearth memories of that journey – his first glimpse of gas lamps (looking like 'souls in hell') and the sight of his youthful mother naked.

> **Background and early years**

From specific biographical data, Freud derived such ideas as the determining role of infant sexuality and the influence of unconscious drives on our behaviour. When Freud's self-analysis became the primal case history of psychoanalysis, his life history acquired a quasi-mythical resonance. In 1935, in the postscript to his scientific self-portrait, he attempted to play down interest in his private life: 'This Autobiographical Study shows how psychoanalysis came to be the whole content of my life and rightly assumes that no personal experiences of mine are of any interest in comparison to my relations with that science.'[2] But a clear separation of the personality from the work cannot be achieved for psychoanalysis goes to work, in an area previously only occupied by art, where details of individual life take on general significance. Freud's postscript underlines the all-importance of his own 'relations with that science': for us today the live issue remains the relations of psychoanalysis to science, and the power of the founder's image continues to be linked with the continuing

---

[1] S.E. XXI.259.

[2] S.E. XX.71.

dispute over the scientific credentials of psychoanalysis. One way to examine this is biographically, simply by following Freud's own background and scientific development.

There are certain general historical aspects of this background that undoubtedly affected Freud profoundly; one of them was that his family was Jewish. Their migration to Vienna in the middle of the nineteenth century was part of a general influx of Jews into the capital of the Austro-Hungarian Empire. Freud was brought up non-religiously, but this did not mean he was totally assimilated into gentile society as an adult. The endemic low-key antisemitism in Viennese society (which was to swell into the triumphal Nazism of the 1930s) hindered Freud's academic and medical career and never allowed him to forget his racial origins. To be Jewish meant to be permanently under threat of attack. Freud speaks of his father's account of having his hat knocked off by a gentile and being ordered to make way. One effect of this image of his father meekly picking up his hat from the road was that Freud resolved never to be so docile himself. For to be Jewish also meant to be a permanent outsider and this was an obstacle that Freud was to turn to his own advantage. 'Because I was a Jew I found myself free from many prejudices which restricted others in the use of their intellect… ' [3]

Studies in neurology, medicine and psychiatry

Freud studied medicine, but as a young graduate without a clear idea of his future career his first preference was for physiological research in the laboratory of Ernst Brücke at Vienna University. Together with Du Bois-Reymond and Ludwig, Brücke had belonged to 'Helmholtz's School of Medicine', a scientific group who revolutionized nineteenth century physiology. Their prime tenet was that all forces within the organism should be explained by chemical or physical causes inherent in matter and reducible to the force of attraction and repulsion; they opposed any resort to the pseudo-mystical 'vital forces' so popular at the time. Freud had accepted their principles and was to develop his own subsequent theories on that basis, though, like Brücke, he modified their determinism through the introduction of evolutionary concepts.

Freud's initial research under Brücke was the structure of spinal nerve cells in Petromyzon, a primitive type of fish, and it

---

[3] S.E. XX.274.

became his first scientific publication, in 1877.[4] It was followed by a further investigation of the subject in 1878. Freud's observations indicated that the spinal ganglion cells of this primitive fish were not radically different from those of higher animals, as had been thought – a significant contribution to current knowledge of the evolution of the nervous system. Even after receiving his medical degree, he carried on working in Brücke's laboratory. However, he came to realise that there was no early prospect of making money in this field. When, in 1882 Freud met and fell in love with a young woman from Hamburg named Martha Bernays, he decided that to establish himself financially in order to marry he would have to go into private practice.

Freud began by studying surgery and spent a couple of years as resident doctor at the General Hospital in Vienna, initially in Nothnagel's Division of Internal Medicine. But practical medicine and daily hospital work failed to arouse his interest. He continued to follow his predilection for anatomical research: in 1879 he had published a paper on his discovery of a new method of staining speciments of nerve tissue to prepare them for microscopic examination.[5] He made brain anatomy and pathology his speciality. It was not until 31 March 1881 that he brought himself to complete his medical studies and belatedly receive his doctorate in medicine. Part of 1883 was spent working in Meynert's psychiatric clinic: from this experience he emerged unenthusiastic about this aspect of medicine as well. One reason for this was the mechanical practice of categorizing psychiatric disorders according to their physical symptoms and to the patient's hereditary tendencies.[6] This standardized approach left no room for originality or imagination and Freud had to turn elsewhere in search of intellectual challenge.

In 1884 Freud was hunting for new discoveries to make his name. One line of investigation concerned the properties of the still relatively unknown drug, cocaine, which he published in the paper 'On Coca'.[7] But because of his failure to follow up tests on

[4] Freud S. Über den Ursprung der hinteren Nervenwurzeln im Rückenmarke von Ammocoetes (Petromyzon Planeri). *Sitzungsber. Akad. Wis. Wien (Math.-Naturwiss. Kl.)* 3 Abt., No. 75 (1877), pp. 15-2

[5] Freud S. Notiz über eine Methode zur anatomischen Präparation des Nervensystems. *Zbl. med. Wiss.*, No. 17 (1879), p.468f.

[6] Hirschmüller A. *Freuds Begegnung mit der Psychiatrie: Von der Hirnmythologie zur Neurosenlehre*. Tübingen: Edition Diskord, 1991, passim.

[7] Freud S. Über Coca. *Zbl. ges. Ther.*, No.2 (1884), pp.289-314.

its application to eye surgery, it was left to Koller to reap the glory of that discovery. In 1885 Freud received a travelling scholarship and went to Paris to study under Jean-Martin Charcot at the Salpêtrière. At this period Charcot had an international reputation in neurology for his characterisation of disorders and above all for his observation of hysteria. It was under his charismatic influence that Freud's interest turned towards psychopathology. Over the next decade he was also to study the use of hypnosis.

However, he still faced the practical problem of marriage and making a living.

'The talking cure'

After a four-year engagement (imposed by poverty and his fiancée's mother), Freud finally married in 1886 and set up in private practice in Vienna. During the first years of married life, Freud also occupied the post of director of the neurological department in Max Kassowitz's Institute for Children's Diseases and in this capacity he continued his work on cerebral anatomy, publishing papers on children's paralyses in 1891 and 1893. Of his early monographs, the one which best indicates his future work is *On Aphasia* of 1891.[8] This critique of existing theories of aphasia, primarily those of Wernicke and Lichtheim, attacked the 'brain mythology' that mental functions can be exactly located in specific areas of the brain. In place of this excessively mechanical explanation, Freud proposed a more complex, less direct system of interaction between anatomy and psychology, or, in this case, between brain and language.[9]

The aphasia study was dedicated to Dr Josef Breuer. Fourteen years older than Freud and a well-established doctor, Breuer was Freud's friend and benefactor during the 1880s, and in the 1890s his collaborator. On his return from Paris in 1886 Freud had delivered two lectures to the Vienna Medical Society on the disputed topic of male hysteria, and wrote a comparative study of organic paralysis and hysterical paralysis. In 1895 Breuer and Freud together published their *Studies in Hysteria*. In later years Freud credited Breuer (and his patient Anna O., the first case in the book), with the discovery of psychoanalysis. It was in fact

[8] Freud S. *Zur Auffassung der Aphasien*. Vienna: 1891

[9] Solms M. & Saling M. On Psychoanalysis and Neuroscience: Freud's Attitude to the Localizationist Tradition. *Int. J.Psycho-Anal.* (1986) 67, 397-416

Anna O. (Bertha Pappenheim) who devised what she termed 'the talking cure'.[10]

Wedding photograph of Freud and Martha, 1886

Freud was first to use the word 'psychoanalysis' in 1896, but a favourable review of *Studies in Hysteria* in late 1895 spoke of 'surgery of the mind' *(Seelenchirurgie)* and referred to it as 'the kind of psychology used by the poets'.[11] This comment corresponded with Freud's own confession that it struck him as strange that 'the case histories I write should read like short stories and that, as one might say, they lack the serious stamp of science'.[12] It is significant that the review was written by a professor of the History of Literature and a theatre director, for throughout its subsequent history, psychoanalysis has probably been more enthusiastically championed by scholars of literature and creative writers than by the medical profession, for its explicatory attraction is far more immediately apparent than its therapeutic efficacy.

---

[10] S.E. II.30.

[11] Jones E. *Sigmund Freud: Life and Work*. London: The Hogarth Press. Vol.1. (1953) pp.278-9.

[12] S.E. II.160.

In the first years of his private practice as a neurologist, Freud had found himself treating numerous neurotic patients. He had tried many of the therapies available at the time, such as electrotherapy, massage or baths, but the only technique that had aroused his enthusiasm was hypnotic suggestion. In 1889 he had travelled to Nancy to study the work of the outstanding practioners of hypnotherapy, Liébeault and and his pupil Bernheim. However, when his own hypnotic cures were eventually followed by relapses, the method revealed its limitations. Now the 'talking cure' or Breuer's 'cathartic method' appeared to offer a viable alternative and Freud began listening attentively to the patient's own account of his or her ailment and observing the concomitant re-enactment of the trauma that had triggered it.

Years later, in *On the History of the Psycho-Analytic Movement*, Freud spoke of 'the unforgotten advice of my master, Charcot: to look at the same things again and again until they themselves begin to speak'.[13] In his progress towards psychoanalysis during the mid 1890s, Freud only gradually abandoned suggestion and hypnotism, as he became more convinced that the hidden traumas he was seeking would 'speak for themselves'. In the initial stages of the therapy passive observation replaced manipulation and coercion: the patient was encouraged to remember and his or her accounts would inevitably wander, apparently at random, over the past, or 'free associate'. Listening to these accounts, Freud became convinced that neuroses were the consequences of sexual traumas. In his effort to discover the origin, he felt that the key events were being suppressed or repressed; relaxed free-association appeared to offer a way past the barrier.

Family and friendships

During the period between 1886 and 1895 Freud's personal life had also changed radically: the lone researcher became a family man. His wife Martha bore him six children in eight years, three daughters and three sons. During that period he led the traditional life of a Viennese doctor: the domain of the household and nursery remained under his wife's jurisdiction, assisted by servants. Her lively-minded unmarried sister Minna Bernays lived with the family from 1895 on, and, during Freud's period of comparative isolation, she was to provide him with intellectual companion-

---

13 S.E. XIV.22.

ship. It was after his last daughter Anna had been born in 1895, and his father had died in 1896, that he began evolving the theoretical basis of psychoanalysis against the background of his own self-analysis and in an atmosphere of intellectual and emotional strain which one historian has termed a 'creative illness'.[14]

The Freud family c.1898. From left to right: front row, Sophie, Anna and Ernst. Middle row, Oliver, Martha and Minna. Back row, Martin and Sigmund Freud

The hidden evolution of his ideas was to be revealed only by the posthumous publication of his letters to his friend Wilhelm Fliess. It was at that time that Freud's friendship with Breuer was giving way to antagonism, perhaps in part founded on the burden of an unpayable debt to this paternal benefactor, but chiefly on Breuer's reluctance to endorse Freud's sexual aetiology of hysteria. He was replaced in Freud's affections by the Berlin ear, nose and throat specialist Wilhelm Fliess, a man of his own age, with whom Freud kept up an intense correspondence during the 1890s. This relationship was to be the chief outlet for Freud's speculation over these years. When Freud embarked on his self-analysis, Fliess was the essential recipient of his insights, both in letters and at their occasional meetings which they termed 'congresses', and it was

---

[14] Ellenberger H.F. *The Discovery of the Unconscious: The History and Evolution of Dynamic Psychiatry.* New York: Basic Books. pp.447-8.

for his eyes that Freud wrote the uncompleted 'Project for a Scientific Psychology' in 1895, his last attempt to construct a single all-embracing theoretical structure that would reconcile mental and physical phenomena.[15]

At the turn of the century, when this friendship too declined into recriminations, with Fliess accusing Freud of appropriating certain of his ideas (such as bisexuality) without due acknowledgment, it seemed as if a pattern of friend becoming foe were being set. It was to be repeated a decade later in Freud's relations with Jung. The fact that each of these friendships involved intellectual collaboration and that its breakdown was connected with a theoretical dispute is a further indication of how inseparable were Freud's private and scientific lives. It also underlines the vital importance of sexuality for Freudian theory, since Jung's chief transgression was to have questioned the sexual origin of neuroses. For without it psychology would lose its direct instinctual link to biology and physical science, and consequently risk falling prey to a tendency Freud constantly fought against, to construct a hermetic system.

Beginnings of psycho-analysis and the psycho-analytical movement

When Freud first embarked on the talking cure, his patients repeatedly presented him with memories of sexual traumas in childhood that he initially believed to be the source of their neuroses. But in 1897 he reported a radical change (and one that is still a source of controversy today). He ceased crediting these accounts, attributing them to the patients' fantasy instead. Henceforth his therapy would set aside the question of the objective reality of a patient's memories and concentrate on the nature of their psychic reality. Critics have asserted that this disregarded real abuses and devalued the patient's actual grievances. But Freud's field of research had shifted from social facts to their psychic ramifications, the reworkings and distortions of memories. This took psychoanalysis out of the realm of history into a new cultural sphere, where dream, fantasy and imagination were to be annexed to a scientific psychology.

In his own memories of the 1890s, Freud was later to speak of years in the wilderness, a tale of intellectual isolation. It is true that he was attacked by the Vienna medical establishment for

---

[15] S.E. 1:283-397.

his early papers on hysteria; it is also true that, as a Jew in a Catholic culture, he always felt the opposition of the conservatives as a spur. Later, there was never to be a shortage of scientists and laymen to express their outrage at his theories and they certainly outnumbered his supporters, but at this period he had more to fear from mockery and indifference. Nevertheless, neither childhood sexuality nor unconscious drives were conceptual innovations, nor was he the first to take dreams seriously. For example, Hughlings Jackson, his mentor for the aphasia study, had already stated: 'Find out all about dreams, and you will have found out all about insanity.'[16]

It was with the provocatively entitled *The Interpretation of Dreams* that Freud definitively flung down his gauntlet to orthodox psychology. Later he spoke of this work as a delayed reaction to the death of his father. The essential theme was that dreams represented the distorted fulfilment of an infantile wish: 'It seems to me that biologically the dream life proceeds altogether from the relics of the prehistoric period (age one to three), the same period that is the source of the unconscious, and the sole one that contains the aetiology of the psychoneuroses; the period for which there is normally an amnesia analogous to that of hysteria.'[17] Furthermore, it was in *The Interpretation of Dreams* that Freud first expounded the Oedipus complex, the desire (which must be repressed and overcome) of the child for the parent of the opposite sex.

As a Privat-Dozent, promoted in 1902 to Professor Extraordinarius, Freud was entitled to lecture at Vienna University and it was through the interest aroused by these lectures that he gathered together a small group of followers. In 1902 they founded the 'Wednesday Psychological Society' to discuss his ideas. This small discussion group composed of both laymen and doctors was later to develop into the Vienna Psychoanalytical Society. At the same time several of his key works during the early years of the century (notably *The Psychopathology of Everyday Life* (1901), *Jokes and their Relation to the Unconscious* (1905) and *Three Essays on the Theory of Sexuality* (1905)) gradually spread his ideas to a wider public outside medical circles.

---

[16] Jones E. *Sigmund Freud: Life and Work*. London: The Hogarth Press. Vol.1. (1953). p.390.

[17] See letter from Sigmund Freud to Wilhelm Fliess, March 10, 1898. In: Jones E. *Sigmund Freud: Life and Work*. London: The Hogarth Press. Vol.1. (1953). p.391.

Freud was eager to break out of the Viennese Jewish-intellectual ghetto in which he lived, and consequently he welcomed the news from the Burghölzli asylum in Switzerland that the eminent psychiatrist Eugen Bleuler and a young assistant, Carl Jung, had begun applying his ideas. In the following years a friendship developed between Jung and Freud, who came to look upon the younger man as his 'Crown Prince', destined to be his intellectual successor. Soon other important foreign followers appeared, including two other assistants from Burghölzli, Karl Abraham and Max Eitingon, also the Hungarian Sándor Ferenczi and Freud's future biographer, the Welshman Ernest Jones. In 1908 the first international psychoanalytical conference was held in Salzburg. The following year Clark University in Massachusetts invited Freud and his colleagues to deliver a series of lectures. This resulted in Freud's single brief visit to the United States, where psychoanalysis was to gain such widespread popularity – and notoriety – in the following years.

Gradually the groups and publications which practised and diffused Freud's ideas took shape. The Vienna Psychoanalytical Society was to be the prototype for numerous other psychoanalytical groups abroad. These formed an international organization that over the course of the next two decades evolved rules and structures and produced publications. As Freud's ideas first began to be popularized in various crude guises, pseudo-analysts proliferated to exploit the fashion. It was necessary for the growing profession to define what made a psychoanalyst and to formalize its relationship to the medical establishment. Freud was always clear that psychoanalysis was not a branch of psychiatry and that analysts did not require a medical training. However, many early followers were medically qualified and in certain countries, most notably the USA, the new institutes of psychoanalysis insisted on medical training for their members. Indeed, one of the grounds for Freud's notorious anti-Americanism was that insistence, in plain contradiction to his own conviction that psychoanalysis was an independent branch of psychology and that it should not be involved in the clinical and normative functions of psychiatric medicine. It was not until the 1920s that the tradition of psychoanalysts undergoing a formal training analysis was established. Until then some had received no analysis at all, others only a very perfunctory one: the basic requirement had merely been a close association with Freud's work.

Some of the questions that these beginnings raised, notably the 'unscientific' nature of psychoanalytic theory and practice, came to a head in the 1920s with the legal action brought against Freud's follower Theodor Reik for 'quackery', and this affair prompted Freud to write his refutation of the accusations in *The Question of Lay Analysis* (1926). However, the dispute had its roots in the increasing specialization of science and medicine and the restriction of access to their respective technologies. Even though psychoanalysis subsequently established its own restrictive hierarchies and power structure, there is no sign that this initial antipathy of the older sciences to what they regarded as an interloper has ceased; on the contrary, the struggle is entering a new phase with the present promotion of chemotherapy and the increasing stress laid nowadays upon the genetic and physiological dimensions of mental disorder.

From the very beginning, even in the *Studies in Hysteria*, Freud deliberately went beyond the scientific pale in his concern with the subject's own narrative. Instead of observing dispassionately, he paid attention to their voice and meanings. This seemed to follow the traditions of textual criticism rather than medical practice. And it was Greek literature that provided the source for the Oedipus complex; literary studies, such as *Delusions and and a Memory of his Childhood* (1910), became standard sources of psychoanalytical theory. Beyond that the theory spilt over into anthropological speculation in *Totem and Taboo* (1913). All these and many other such instances were seen as classificatory crimes or sins against the regimentation of both the physical and the human sciences.

Freud repeatedly acknowledged that many of his key ideas, such as repression or the unconscious, or infantile sexuality, had already been expressed by artists or philosophers, and that his own merit was not so much his originality but rather his ability to formulate and investigate these concepts systematically. As he stated, 'it is one thing to give utterance to an idea once or twice in the form of a passing aperçu, and quite another to mean it seriously – to take it literally and pursue it in the face of every contradictory detail, and to win it a place among accepted truths'.[18]

---

[18] S.E. XIV.15.

Culture and the development of psycho-analysis

Although Freud's life was almost entirely devoted to his work, he did begin to find space, as he emerged from relative poverty, for his two favourite recreations of travel and collecting antiquities. Like most educated men of his time, Freud had had a classical education: he saw himself as a man of the Mediterranean, and Italy was his favourite holiday destination.[19] He wrote of both his first trip to Rome in 1901 and to Athens in 1904 as breakthroughs into a new phase of his life. Through the discoveries of such archaeologists as Heinrich Schliemann, Arthur Evans and Leonard Woolley, he was able to experience vicariously the pleasure of unearthing the buried past. The growing collection of antiquities that decorated his study and consulting room in Vienna were a transfiguration of stages in the development of the individual and of culture in general.

Of the early followers, Jung shared Freud's involvement with mythology, but was to arrive at a radically different interpretation of its significance. In 1912-13 he split with Freud: because of their friendship this was a bitter blow for both men. He was not the first to abandon psychoanalysis because of doctrinal differences; among the earliest members of the Wednesday Society, Alfred Adler and Wilhelm Stekel also 'defected'. As a result of this defection, in 1912 a small group of loyal members was formed (Ernest Jones, Sándor Ferenczi, Hanns Sachs, Karl Abraham, Otto Rank and, later, Max Eitingon) as a 'secret committee' to safeguard Freudian psychoanalysis from dilution or distortion. The idea was not Freud's but it appealed to him, for he was eager to shift the organizational burdens of the psychoanalytical movement on to younger members. In the 1920s the committee ceased functioning, but its conspiratorial nature had set an awkward precedent. Psychoanalysis in the early years was always embattled, but had developed in response defensive strategies that attracted as much antagonism as they combated.

During these years Freud continued to lead an orderly and regular personal life. The First World War disrupted the pattern for him as for everyone else. The initial general jingoism soon subsided and was replaced by anxiety and material shortages. Freud had always been troubled by superstitious premonitions of his own premature death. Now, however, with his three sons, Martin, Ernst and Oliver, all in active service, he was forced to

---

[19] Tögel C. *Berggasse – Pompeii und zurück.* Tübingen: Edition Diskord (1989). pp.37-8.

face the real possibility of their particular deaths among the general butchery. These considerations produced such papers as *Thoughts for the Times on War and Death* and *Mourning and Melancholia*. Of necessity, the business of the international psychoanalytical movement fell into abeyance. However, in compensation Freud was left with more time to devote to his own work. One result was that during the years from 1915 to 1917 he saw to the publication of his professorial lectures at Vienna University – *Introductory Lectures on Psycho-Analysis*. He was also able to produce an important series of theoretical works, the *Papers on Metapsychology*.

The end of the war meant the end of the Austro-Hungarian Empire in which Freud had grown up; he now found himself a citizen of a small and starving country. Relatives and friends abroad helped him and his family through the hardship of post-war poverty and during the 1920s he took on an increasing number of English and American analysands whose hard currency payments helped protect the family income against inflation.

When the international movement resumed work, with its first post-war conference in The Hague in 1920, Freud attended, accompanied by his youngest daughter Anna. She was the only one of his six children to have shown a real interest in psychoanalysis and was now training to become an analyst herself. Her older sisters had by this time both married, and it was also in 1920 that one of them, Sophie, died, apparently from an infection following an abortion. Curiously, whether emotionally exhausted by the war years or compensated by the survival of his three sons, Freud mourned her less than he did her youngest son who died in infancy three years later. His death coincided with what was in effect Freud's own death sentence, the appearance of cancer of the jaw, shortly before the boy's death from miliary tuberculosis.[20]

Freud was an addictive cigar smoker – he began at the age of twenty-four – sometimes having up to twenty a day. Occasionally he also smoked a pipe. In 1894 he attempted to give it up for health reasons, but he soon relapsed. During the 1930s, when he was forced to cut down drastically, again for health reasons, he complained that because he could not smoke, he could hardly

---

[20] 'I don't think I have ever experienced such grief; perhaps my own sickness contributes to the shock. [...]... fundamentally everything has lost its meaning for me.' Freud to Kata and Lajos Lévy. June 11, 1923. In: Ernst L. Freud (Ed.) *Letters of Sigmund Freud* (Transl. Tania & James Stern). New York: Basic Books (1960).

write.[21] There is no doubt that this addiction was the cause of the cancer which developed in the twenties and which necessitated regular operations from 1923 onwards. In two serious operations that year the surgeon Hans Pichler removed the infected part of Freud's jaw and soft palate. For the rest of his life he was condemned to wear an oral prosthesis to enable him to talk, eat or smoke more or less normally. There is no doubt that it was Pichler's subsequent prompt excision of all threatening neoplasms that extended Freud's life far beyond the five years or so allowed by a more pessimistic prognosis. Over the next fifteen years, which included thirty operations, innumerable consultations and constant treatment, Pichler was able to contain the disease, but at a high cost to the patient who stoically endured repeated painful surgery and the perpetual discomfort of successive ill-fitting prostheses.[22] Even when Varaztad Kazanjian, a specialist of international renown, created a prosthesis for him at great expense in 1931, the alleviation of his suffering was only temporary.

Return to the origins

In the early 1920s Freud enlarged the theoretical work that he had termed his metapsychology. This included descriptions of psychical processes at various conceptual levels (their development, their relationship to each other and their interaction). Two outstanding works of this period were *Beyond the Pleasure Principle* (1920), which introduced the hypothesis of a death drive as counterpoint to the pleasure principle, and *The Ego and the Id* (1923), which charted the component forces of mental activity.

In its speculative aspect metapsychology bordered on philosophy and Freud was to speak of his early fascination with philosophy and his suppression of that tendency. Above all, it was cultural theory that now attracted Freud: 'My interest, after making a lifelong détour through the natural sciences, medicine and psychotherapy, returned to the cultural problems which had fascinated me long before, when I was a youth scarcely old enough for thinking.'[23] There were numerous determinants for this. Firstly, it had always remained an integral part of psychoana-

---

[21] Molnar M. (Ed.) *The Diary of Sigmund Freud 1929-1939: A Record of the Final Decade* London: The Hogarth Press (1992). p.53 & passim.

[22] see Pichler Notes (Freud Museum: Typescript) & Romm S. *The Unwelcome Intruder: Freud's Struggle with Cancer*. New York: Praeger Publishers (1983).

[23] S.E. XX.72.

lytical theory, particularly in such works as *Totem and Taboo*; secondly, the world war and subsequent political upheavals focussed attention on the disruptions in civilization and cried out for some sort of explanation. A third reason is provided by Freud's own situation; old age and bad health had severely restricted his social life, and speculation remained a compensatory link with world affairs. And there were still scores to settle. One of them, with the old enemy, religion, was dealt with in *The Future of an Illusion* (1927), a debunking rationale of belief. Another, the ideal of human progress, was subjected to sceptical scrutiny in *Civilization and its Discontents* (1930).

Events in the following years were to prove that this scepticism was more than justified. Hitler's rise to power in 1933 spelled Austria's doom, although Nazism was precariously held at bay until 1938 by the Austro-fascist regimes of Dollfuss and Schuschnigg. Freud's general health declined during these years. No longer could he leave Vienna during the summer as he needed to be within constant reach of his doctors, particularly Pichler. But he could still escape from the dark apartment on Berggasse by spending the summer months in a villa on the outskirts of the city. The violent upsurge of antisemitism was reflected in his work; in 1934 he began working on *Moses and Monotheism*, a study of Judaism which attempted to relate anti-semitism to contradictions surrounding the founding Moses figure and to the ambiguous character of the deity. He was to finish the work in 1938, in England, himself a refugee from the barbaric forces whose origin he had been trying to identify.

When Austria submitted to Hitler's invasion in March 1938, Freud and his family were trapped. Both as a Jew and an ideological opponent whose books had already been ritually burnt by the Nazis in 1933, Freud was in mortal danger. But influential friends, above all William Bullitt, Princess Marie Bonaparte and Ernest Jones, immediately began diplomatic manoeuvres on his behalf, and after three months of negotiation for exit and entry visas (a period which included house searches and Anna Freud's brief detainment by the Gestapo), they were able to flee the country in June 1938 and settle in London.[24]

Anna Freud was to resume her life's work in child therapy

---

[24] see Molnar op. cit. pp.228-239.

Freud on his arrival at his first London address, 39 Elsworthy Road, with his daughter Mathilde and his biographer Ernest Jones

in Britain, but for her father exile offered only a brief respite. Just before he moved from temporary accommodation into his 'last address on this planet' at 20 Maresfield Gardens in September 1938, Freud underwent a final operation.[25] Its consequence was months of pain. By early 1939, after a brief attempt at radiotherapy, it became clear that the cancer was inoperable and incurable. In the summer of 1938 Freud had begun what was to have been a resumé of his life's work, *An Outline of Psycho-Analysis* (1940), but this had to be abandoned unfinished. His last patients were dismissed in July 1939 and fifty-three years after he had first set up as a neurologist in Vienna, he terminated his practice.

[25] see Molnar op. cit. pp.247-248.

In 1930, when he began consulting the young Viennese physician Max Schur, Freud exacted from him the promise not to
subject him to unnecessary suffering. In September, three weeks
after the outbreak of the Second World War, Freud kept Schur to
that promise. Schur administered an overdose of morphine and
on 23 September Freud died.[26]

As for the death of psychoanalysis, sporadic reports have so
far proved premature. While there has been a recent decline in the
popularity of psychoanalysis as therapy in Europe and the United
States, there is an increase of interest in South America and in
former Iron Curtain countries. Meanwhile, numerous other forms
of treatment, most founded on some aspect of Freudian thinking,
have absorbed a growing demand for psychotherapy. The survival of practice and theory are not necessarily congruent:
Freudian theory continues to influence other spheres of thought.
Freud's merit (and transgression) was to have extrapolated a
theory of mental processes into a general explanation of human
conduct and culture. The initial problem had been the vexed question of origins. How did conscious thought and cultural activity
emerge from their biological and physical source? What are the
fundamental laws that underlie the variety of mental activity? His
theoretical themes were variations on the 'mighty and primordial
melody of the instincts'[27]: in the end, he speculated, 'all our pro-
visional ideas in psychology will presumably some day be based
on an organic substructure'.[28] In the course of his quest, Freud
developed a set of brilliant theoretical strategies, such as the
interpretation of dreams, the pleasure principle and wish fulfilment. His therapy used transference to mobilize repression and
unconscious mental activity on behalf of the patient. But beyond
that, he created a new framework for understanding the nature
and place of the human subject in the world. His statement of
intent in his *Autobiographical Study* might be read as a description
of his contribution to twentieth century culture: 'I must endeavour
to construct a narrative in which subjective and objective attitudes, biographical and historical interests, are combined in a
new proportion.'[29]

---

[26] Schur M. *Freud: Living and Dying*. London: The Hogarth Press and the Institute of
Psycho-Analysis (1972). pp.407-9, p.529.

[27] S.E. XIV.62.

[28] S.E. XIV.78.

[29] S.E. XX.7.

The life of Sigmund Freud: a brief chronology

1856   Born on 6 May in Freiberg, Moravia

1859   Move from Freiberg to Leipzig
1860   Family settles in Vienna

1865   Enters Leopoldstädter Gymnasium school

1873   Hears essay 'On Nature' (attributed to Goethe) at a lecture
        Decides to study medicine at the University of Vienna

1877   First publications, on intersexuality in eels and on Petromyzon

1881   Graduates as doctor of medicine
1882   Engaged to Martha Bernays
1882-5 Works in Vienna General Hospital
1884-7 Researches into the clinical uses of cocaine
1885-6 Studies under Charcot at the Salpêtrière, Paris. Charcot provides new
        insight into hysteria and uses hypnosis
1886   Sets up private practice; marries Martha Bernays
1887   Treats nervous diseases in his practice; introduces hypnotic suggestion
1891   Writes *On Aphasia*, about language disorders and neurology
1893-6 Works with Josef Breuer on case histories (including that of 'Anna O')
        which later become *Studies on Hysteria* (1895)
1895   Drafts *Project for a Scientific Psychology*, an attempt to work out a
        psychology based on neurological terms
1896   First use of the term 'psychoanalysis'; death of his father
1897   Freud's self-analysis begins, leading to the abandonment of the trauma
        theory of neurosis (developed with Breuer), recognition of infantile
        sexuality and the Oedipus complex
1899   December, *The Interpretation of Dreams* published. Freud's favourite book
        containing dozens of dream analyses on the way to 'the royal road to
        the unconscious'
1901   *The Psychopathology of Everyday Life*: introduction of 'Freudian slip'
1902   Founding of the Wednesday Psychological Society

A general historical chronology 1856-1939

1856	Treaty of San Stefano ends Crimean War
	George Bernard Shaw and Woodrow Wilson born
	Heinrich Heine dies
1859	Darwin publishes *The Origin of Species*
	Building of Suez Canal begun. Austria at war with Piedmont
	Battles of Magenta and Solferino
1863	International Red Cross set up at Geneva
1865	Mendel discovers the laws of heredity
	Lincoln assassinated
1866-7	Invention of dynamite by Alfred Nobel
1860s	Bismarck engineers movement towards German unification
1868	First plastic (celluloid) produced by John W. Hyatt
	Dry cell battery patented by Georges Leclanché
1869	Franco-Prussian War
1874	Safety bicycle invented by H.J. Lawson
1875-6	Telephone invented by Alexander Graham Bell
1876	Internal combustion engine designed by N.A. Otto
1877	Edison's phonograph. Russo-Turkish War
1881	Assassination of Tsar Alexander II
	Robert Koch discovers tuberculosis bacillus
1883	Carbon-filament light produced by T.A. Edison and Joseph Swan
1885	Carl Benz and Gottlieb Daimler construct first motor car
1886	Statue of Liberty unveiled
1889	Mayerling Affair: heir to Austrian throne commits suicide
1894	The Dreyfus Affair: a wave of antisemitism sweeps France
1895	First public cinema performance in Paris
	Röntgen discovers X-rays
	Pocket camera produced by Kodak
1897	Karl Lueger, antisemitic mayor of Vienna, elected
1898	First commercial wireless telegram transmitted
1901	Blood groups discovered by Karl Landsteiner
1902	Lenin writes *What is to be Done?*
1903	Wright Brothers' first powered flight at Kitty Hawk

► *page 125*

The life of Sigmund Freud *continued*

1905 *Three Essays on the Theory of Sexuality* ; 'Dora' case published (although the case dates from 1899); *Jokes and their Relation to the Unconscious*

1906 Freud becomes friend and colleague of the Swiss adherent of psychoanalysis, Carl Gustav Jung

1908 Salzburg: first international meeting of psychoanalysts

1909 Freud and Jung travel to the USA and give the Clark Lectures: first lectures on psychoanalysis in America. (Freud is not enamoured of America; sees it as a 'big mistake')

1912 Jung returns to USA

1912-13 Freud publishes *Totem and Taboo* which explores how culture and society are rooted in the prohibition against incest, an assertion contrary to the development of Jung's studies

1914 Secession of Jung from the official psychoanalytic movement

1915-17 *Introductory Lectures* given

1919 Freud observes soldiers traumatized by the war

1920 Death of Freud's daughter, Sophie
Publishes *Beyond the Pleasure Principle* which introduces new theories of the 'compulsion to repeat' and the concept of the 'death instinct', as well as a revision of the 1900 theory of dreams as wish fulfilments

1921 Publishes *Group Psychology and the Analysis of the Ego*

1923 *The Ego and the Id*. Deals with a new account of the structure of the mind, revising the one to be found in *The Interpretation of Dreams*.
Freud diagnosed as suffering from cancer

1926 *Inhibitions, Symptoms and Anxiety*. Freud makes anxiety the cornerstone of his developmental theory

1927 *The Future of an Illusion*. A consideration of the origins of religion. Freud, here, explicitly states his atheism

1930 *Civilization and its Discontents*. A profoundly pessimistic account of the irreconcilability of personal drives and the demands of society

1932 *Why War?*

1933 Freud's books, along with other psychoanalytical works, publicly burned by the Nazis in Berlin

1936 Freud's 80th birthday. Honoured by the Royal Society in Britain who make him a Foreign Member

1938 Nazis invade Austria. Freud and his family manage to get exit visas
Moves to 20 Maresfield Gardens, London NW3. Continues work, seeing patients and finishing *Moses and Monotheism* and *An Outline of Psychoanalysis*

1939 On 23 September Freud dies in London

A general history *continued*

1904	Russo-Japanese War
	Pavlov receives Nobel Prize for work on digestion
1905	First Russian Revolution crushed. Sinn Fein founded.
	Einstein's Theory of Relativity. Binet's first intelligence test
1908	Austria-Hungary annexes Bosnia-Herzegovina
	Picasso and Braque found Cubism
1912	War in the Balkans
1913	First Charlie Chaplin film. Proust's *À la recherche du temps perdu* published
1914	Passports made compulsory for foreign travel
1914-18	First World War
1917	Russian Revolution
1919	'Spartakus' revolt brutally suppressed in Germany
1921	Founding of BBC
1922	Mussolini rises to power. Joyce's *Ulysses* published
1923	Great Depression in Germany and Austria
	Ruhr occupied by France and Belgium
1926	General Strike in Britain
1927	First Five Year Plan in Soviet Union.
	First solo trans-Atlantic flight by Lindberg
1929	Stock Market crash on Wall Street
	Alexander Fleming discovers penicillin
1932	James Chadwick discovers the neutron
1933	Hitler gains power. Reichstag fire and book burnings in Germany
1934	Dollfuss, Austrian Chancellor, murdered by Nazis
1935	Leucotomy introduced by Egas Moniz
	Antisemitic Nuremberg Laws passed in Germany
1936	Beginning of Spanish Civil War. First BBC television transmission
1938	Munich Agreement; Nazis invade Austria
1939	Outbreak of Second World War. Nylon stockings invented

Select bibliography of Freud's works

1893 'On the Psychical Mechanism of Hysterical Phenomena Preliminary Communication' (with Breuer) in *Studies on Hysteria* (1895)

1895 'Project for a Scientific Psychology'

1900 *The Interpretation of Dreams* (published late 1899: copyright date 1900)

1901 *The Psychopathology of Everyday Life*

1905 'Fragment of an Analysis of a Case of Hysteria ('Dora')'
Three Essays on the Theory of Sexuality
Jokes and their Relation to the Unconscious

1907 *Delusions and Dreams in Jensen's 'Gradiva'*
'Creative Writers and Day-dreaming'

1909 'Analysis of a Phobia in a Five-Year-Old ('Little Hans')'
'Notes upon a Case of Obsessional Neurosis ('The Rat Man')

1910 *Leonardo da Vinci and a Memory of his Childhood*

1911 *Psychoanalytic Notes on an Autobiographical Account of a Case of Paranoia* (The Schreber case)

1912 'The Dynamics of Transference'

1913 *Totem and Taboo*

1914 *The Moses of Michelangelo*
'On Narcissism: An Introduction'

1915 'Instincts and their Vicissitudes'
'Repression'
'The Unconscious'

1916-17 *Introductory Lectures on Psychoanalysis*

1917 'Mourning and Melancholia'

1918 'From the History of an Infantile Neurosis ('The Wolf Man')'

1919 'The Uncanny'

1920 *Beyond the Pleasure Principle*

1921 *Group Psychology and the Analysis of the Ego*

1923 *The Ego and the Id*

1926 *Inhibitions, Symptoms and Anxiety*
The Question of Lay Analysis

1927 *The Future of an Illusion*
'Fetishism'

1930 *Civilization and its Discontents*

1931 'Female Sexuality'

1933 *New Introductory Lectures on Psychoanalysis*

1939 *Moses and Monotheism: Three Essays*

1940 *An Outline of Psychoanalysis*

Further reading

Ronald W. Clark *Freud: The Man and The Cause*, Granada, London, 1982

Henri F. Ellenberger *The Discovery of the Unconscious: The History and Evolution of Dynamic Psychiatry,* Basic Books, New York, 1970

**Ernst Freud,
Lucie Freud,
Ilse Grubrich-
Simitis** *(eds)* *Sigmund Freud: His Life in Pictures and Words*, André Deutsch, London, 1978

Ernst Freud *(ed)* *Letters of Sigmund Freud*, Basic Books, New York, 1960

Martin Freud *Sigmund Freud: Man and Father,* Jason Aronson, New York, 1983

Peter Gay *Freud: A Life for Our Time*, Dent, London, 1988

H.D. *(Hilda Doolittle)* *Tribute to Freud*, Carcanet, Manchester, 1985

Ernest Jones *The Life and Work of Sigmund Freud,* Penguin Books, Harmondsworth, 1993

J. Laplanche *and*
J.-B. Pontalis *The Language of Psycho-Analysis*, Karnac, London, 1988

**Jeffrey Moussaieff
Masson** *(ed)* *The Complete Letters of Sigmund Freud to Wilhelm Fliess 1887-1904*, Belknap, London, 1985

Michael Molnar *(ed)* *The Diary of Sigmund Freud 1929-1939*, Hogarth, London, 1992

Uwe Henrik Peters *Anna Freud: A Life Dedicated to Children,* Weidenfeld and Nicolson, London, 1985

Philip Rieff *Freud: The Mind of the Moralist*, University of Chicago Press, Chicago and London, 1979

Charles Rycroft *A Critical Dictionary of Psychoanalysis*, Penguin, London, 1972

Max Schur *Freud: Living and Dying*, Hogarth, London, 1972

Frank J. Sulloway *Freud: Biologist of the Mind*, Fontana, London, 1980

Richard Wollheim *Freud*, Fontana, London, 1991

**Elisabeth Young-
Bruehl** *Anna Freud: A Biography,* Summit Books, New York, 1988

The literature on Freud is so vast and various that any selection must leave out many excellent works. The above list is intended only as an introduction, primarily to the historical and biographical background of psychoanalysis. As for Freud's own writings, the fifteen volumes of the Penguin Freud Library will provide the best introduction.

Acknowledgements

This book owes its existence to its co-authors, the staff of the Freud Museum, London: Erica Davies, J. Keith Davies, Michael Molnar, Susan O'Cleary, Ivan Ward.

The following institutions and individuals have also made a contribution.

Firstly, the Freud Museum owes a basic and continual debt of gratitude to the New-Land Foundation whose support has enabled it to continue functioning through difficult times. Thanks must go to the London Management Committee and to Sigmund Freud Archives, as well as to previous staff of the museum, for caring deeply about the preservation of a unique heritage.

For the right to reproduce the Freud copyright photos we thank Mark Paterson and Thomas Roberts and A.W. Freud et al. We also thank Jane Rolo and Book Works for the photograph of Susan Hiller's work.

Museum copyright photos were taken by Nick Bagguley, Ian Ridley and Nigel Bradley, and the plan of the house was drawn by Ian Hay.

We must thank Alexandre Bento and Francisco da Silva, who look after the house and grounds of 20 Maresfield Gardens with such meticulous attention.

We are grateful to those whose interest in Freud and the Freud Museum has contributed both materially and intellectually towards the contents of this book. Particular thanks are due to the experts who have catalogued the collection of antiquities: Anna Lucia d'Agata, Lucilla Burn, Eric Gubel, Roger Keverne and Nick Reeves.

Finally we owe thanks to Ann Scott and to Peter Ayrton and Ruth Petrie of Serpent's Tail for guiding this book into print, and to Sue Lamble for the book's design.

Freud Museum
20 Maresfield Gardens
London NW3 5SX

tel: 020 7435 2002
fax: 020 7431 5452
e-mail: info@freud.org.uk
website: www.freud.org.uk

Index